CONTENTS

CHRISTIAN CRITICISM

A Study of Literary God-Talk

by

© Editions Rodopi N.V., Amsterdam 1976
Printed in the Netherlands
ISBN: 90–6203–379–2

PREFACE

From the galaxy of people who have whetted my mind for things literary and theological I should like to acknowledge my special indebtedness to a few stars who have shown me particular warmth and insight at times when I most needed encouragement. First, I would like to pay respect to Professor Ross Garner, who was kind enough to regard my first embarrassing fumblings with religion and literature as if they were important, for trying to teach me how to write about such matters, all too in vain, with precision and grace. His profound influence on the conduct and content of my mind will be abundantly clear on every page.

Secondly, I would like to pay tribute to my professor, adviser and friend, the late Helen C. White, whose patience and guidance brought me to a deep appreciation of seventeenth-century life and letters. Finally, I would like to mention two theologians, both brothers-in-law, who have kept my awareness of theological matters as keenly honed as they were able: the late Professor Carl Michalson and Professor Paul Clasper. Their imprints on my thinking are probably greater than they ever imagined.

I should like to thank *Language and Style* for permission to include the material (in slightly different form) which makes up Chapter Five. Similarly, I thank *Neuphilologische Mitteilungen* for allowing me to use material contained in Chapters Eight and Ten. Margaret Pyle Hassert deserves particular thanks for her illuminating suggestions and thorough proofreading of the text.

Blue Hill, Maine
August 1974

Chapter One: The Divine Idiom

"If we substitute Anglo-Saxon roots from Greek ones," says John Macquarrie, "the word 'theology' would seem to be equivalent to 'God-talk.' It is a form of discourse professing to speak about God."[1] I find Macquarrie's pungent coinage provocative for at least three reasons. First, its engaging directness bears with it the interesting notion that there is something odd or unusual about the conduct of language when it is used for religious purposes. Macquarrie himself speaks of God-talk as "different from our everyday discoursing about what is going on in the world," and this remark urges me to inquire *how* it is different and what effect this difference might have on my understanding of Christian literature. Is religious language special? Does it really possess a distinctive style or unique behavior of its own that sets it apart from conventional language?

Second, Macquarrie's fusion of Theology's ultimate concern (God) with Literature's very essence (talk) encourages me, at least, to assume that a stronger dialogical partnership between Theology and Literature, one contracted upon a common ground of linguistic concern, would not only be illuminating but obligatory for an adequate understanding of what really "happens" in a religious literary enterprise. After all, if the behavior of God-talk is in fact eccentric, as many theologians, philosophers and linguists maintain today,[2] should literary specialists or even general readers be kept in

1. *God-talk: An Examination of the Language and Logic of Theology* (London: SCM, 1967), p. 11.
2. The acknowledgment of the eccentric nature of religious language was brought on by the challenge of Logical Positivism that religious assertions, because they are empirically unverifiable and analytically irreducible to tautology, make no logical sense. The Positivist view was popularized by A. J. Ayer's *Language, Truth and Logic* (London, 1935). The response to this challenge came from many quarters, as Chapter Three will indicate, but the most significant for my purpose are Ian Ramsey's *Religious Language: An Empirical Placing of Theological Phrases,* 2nd ed. (London: Victor Gollancz, 1946), and I. M. Crombie, *Faith and Logic* (London, 1958), to select a mere two from the vast literature on the subject.

the dark about it? Should they be left alone to continue making *non*-religious accounts of essentially religious activities?

Finally, Macquarrie's term confronts me with my own incompetence. It arouses in me (and, I hope, in others) a strong suspicion that a great number of literary judgments I have been trained to make about Christian works such as the ones I take as models for this study, *Paradise Lost, The Temple,* and Donne's sermons, may well be quite off the mark simply because I have not properly understood the language in which they are written. What follows is a modest first step toward a remedy. It is an attempt to introduce Literature to some of the provocative issues of religious style which up to now have been largely the concern of Theology.

Perhaps the best way to illustrate the structural dissimilarity of God-talk and everyday language is to imagine a potentially religious situation in which everyday language is the order of the day and God-talk has been systematically disallowed. John Wisdom has created a parable which provides exactly such a situation:

> Once upon a time two explorers came upon a clearing in the jungle. In the clearing were growing many flowers and many weeds. One explorer says, 'Some gardener must tend this plot'. The other disagrees, 'There is no gardener.' So they pitch their tents and set a watch. No gardener is seen. So they set up a barbed-wire fence. They electrify it. They patrol with bloodhounds. (For they remember that H. G. Wells' *The Invisible Man* could be both smelt and touched though he could not be seen.) but no shrieks suggest that some intruder has received a shock. No movements of the wire ever betray an invisible climber. The bloodhounds never give a cry. Yet still the Believer is not convinced. 'But there is a gardener, invisible, intangible, insensible to electric shocks, a gardener who has no scent and makes no sound, a gardener who comes secretly to look after the garden which he loves.' At last the Sceptic despairs, 'But what remains of your original assertion? Just how does what you call an invisible, intangible, eternally elusive gardener differ from an imaginary gardener or even from no gardener at all? '[3]

The parable records, among other things, the slow attrition of an

---

3. The rendering of Professor Wisdom's parable that I give here is that of Antony Flew in *New Essays in Philosophical Theology,* ed. A. G. N. Flew and A. MacIntyre (London: SCM, 1955), p. 96. The original version appeared in Wisdom's essay, "Gods," *Logic and Language (First Series),* ed. Antony Flew (Oxford: Basil Blackwell, 1955), pp. 192-3.

essentially theological assertion as it comes under challenge by the impressive force of empirical scrutiny. As experimentation uncovers each new piece of damaging "evidence" against his conviction, the hapless Believer, maneuvered into the position of defending his theological belief in empirical terms, is forced to accommodate the characteristics of his Gardener to meet the challenge. His original theological premise — his "fine brash hypothesis," to use Antony Flew's words — is "killed by inches, the death of a thousand qualifications."[4]

We might assume that once the Sceptic overcomes his exasperation at what he can only see as a perverse obtuseness on the part of the Believer, he will declare a victory for the scientific method and happily dismiss the Invisible Gardener theory as poppycock. But a less positivistic witness to the parable (one willing to acknowledge the existence of immaterial reality) might see that the Believer's position is not necessarily untenable but that it is one played against a linguistically stacked deck. The Believer wants to posit his Gardener as an ultimate explanation for all that occurs in the world — its sustaining antecedent — but the language he agrees to use is one which insists that sense-evidence is the last court of truth-seeking appeal. The Believer, therefore, finds himself engaged in a "language-game" in which his best (indeed only) shots are ruled illegal. His faith-sponsored "evidence" is systematically discounted in favor of sense-sponsored "fact." Had the tables been turned, had the Sceptic been forced to argue his *dis*belief under the rules of God-talk, the jungle encounter might have had an entirely different outcome.

The fundamental lesson that the parable teaches is that the language we speak only *appears* to have a uniform consistency. In many or most circumstances, as Antony Flew points out, "expressions may be grammatically similar and yet logically different."[5] Professor F. Waismann, for example, likes to employ the term "language strata" to describe the difference in *"logical style"* that he contends one feels when one "compares such statements as: a material object statement, a sense-datum statement, a law of nature, a geometric proposition, a statement describing a dream, a

4. *Ibid.*
5. *Logic and Language (First Series),* p. 7.

proverb, and so forth."[6] To this list I would want to add, of course, "a God statement." Whether we term these differences in logical style "language strata" (Waismann), "language-games" (Wittgenstein), "Universes of discourse" (Urban), or "discourse situations" (Macquarrie), the fact remains, as Wittgenstein ultimately discovered, that meaning in language is determined not by rigid referential definition but by *how* (in what logical context) the words are used. The semantic behavior of a particular stratum of language is invariably dictated by a commitment to a logical premise. "Change the logic," says Waismann, "and then the propositions will take on new meanings."[7]

Clearly, no one would knowingly attempt a serious interpretation of a literary specimen without understanding the basis of its logical style, and yet, this happens consistently with God-talk and with predictable interpretive disaster. The reason for God-talk's peculiar vulnerability to misinterpretation can be discovered in what David Crystal calls its " 'analogical' nature: it is capable of being interpreted on two largely independent planes. Both planes can ultimately be conflated in the central notion 'God,' but at any one time, either of the alternative modes of interpretation may be referred to."[8] This interpretive hospitality which God-talk extends precipitatives many hazards. Imagine, for example, Wisdom's positivist Sceptic reading a Christian work but refusing to acknowledge the appropriate rules of its language-game! Imagine him perversely taking Christianity's fundamental dogma, "Christ is the Son of God," as a genealogical statement! Imagine him confronting the doctrine of the Trinity only to deal with it as a proposition of physics! These are, to be sure, extreme examples, but they do illustrate the nature of the mischief that often occurs when utterances of one language-game are interpreted according to rules appropriate to another. We mix language-games at our peril.

Just as important as the sorting out of God-talk from everyday talk in our reading of Christian literature is the attention we

6. F. Waismann, "Language Strata," *Logic and Language (Second Series),* ed. A.G.N. Flew (Oxford: Basil Blackwell, 1966), p. 19.

7. *Ibid.,* p. 21.

8. David Crystal and Derek Davy, *Investigating English Style,* gen. ed., Randolph Quirk, English Language Series (London: Longman's, 1969), p. 167.

pay in our critical judgments not to run at cross purposes with the language-game before us. To explicate a poetic devotion, for example, as though it belonged to the language-game of amorous rapture, aesthetic delight, or even moral discipline may be a personally satisfying exercise, but such an explication should not be offered as an aid to broadening our appreciation or knowledge of the devotion as devotion. What it does, in fact, is to reduce the religious depth of the devotion to fit an inadequately hospitable set of interpretive circumstances. Literary analysis systematically discounts and ignores the religious intention of the Christian texts it considers when it articulates its judgments according to the rules of a language-game specifically structured to make only ethical and aesthetic assessments. An understanding of the principles of God-talk and an application of them to the literary criticism of Christian works can only be therapeutic. At the very least it might force a more honest posture towards the sometimes conflicting claims in religious literature of piety and art.

If Wisdom's Sceptic had been eavesdropping on our discussion up to this point, it is likely that he might have broken in to dismiss what we have been calling God-talk as mere emotive language, perhaps remembering Matthew Arnold's definition of religion as "morality tingled with emotion." In one sense he would be right. God-talk is certainly not in the business of dispensing mere information, if by information we mean factual data about observable phenomena. Indeed, the terms most frequently used to describe God-talk's unique character — "presentational language" (Carl Michalson), "performative language" (J.L. Austin), "discernment-commitment language" (Ian Ramsey), "speech acts" (John Macquarrie) and "speech event" (Gerhard Ebeling) — all seem to emphasize what such language *does* rather than *says*. God-talk seems to strive to do more than inform us; its aim appears to be to *change* us.

The question of God-talk's cognitive status, over and above its obvious conative significance, is an important one, for if religious literature is merely a matter of manipulating subjective feelings, can God-talk claim any anchorage at all in reality? Can it claim to speak of anything beyond the speaker's own attitudes and feelings? Note Ayer's radically empirical challenge:

The theist, like the moralist, may believe that his experiences are cog-

nitive experiences, but, unless he can formulate his 'knowledge' in propositions that are empirically verifiable, we may be sure that he is
deceiving himself. It follows that those philosophers who fill their books
with assertions that they intuitively 'know' this or that moral or religious
'truth' are merely providing material for the psycho-analyst. For no act of
intuition can be said to reveal a truth about any matter of fact unless it
issues in verifiable propositions. And all such propositions are to be in-
corporated in the system of empirical propositions which constitutes
science.[9]

Even a point of view not hostile to religious language, E. L.
Mascall's, concedes that "the word 'God' must have some content
if our statements about God are to be intelligible at all; and if we
say what the content is we are inevitably saying things about
him."[10]

One can speak to this challenge, I think, in a general and a
specific way. The general reply would first of all object to the
loaded definition of "cognition" which Ayer puts forward. It
would retort, as Wisdom's Believer neglected to, that "cognitive
significance," limited to non-subjective knowledge, is a sell-out to
the empirical language-game. If knowledge can be only of observable things, the immaterial reality to which God-talk refers indeed
is nonsense. To defend God-talk, the theist must first defend the
validity of a cognitive significance which is *independent* of empirical data or analytical inference. He would have to promote the
proposition that certain insights or discernments, which admittedly occur in the subjective consciousness, nevertheless qualify as
genuine cognitive inputs. By discernment he would no doubt mean
a kind of interior revelation — when a sudden understanding of
something he has looked at for years floods in upon him, when the
"light dawns" and the familiar abruptly speaks to him as it has
never spoken before.

The novelist Walker Percy writes knowingly of such discernment when he describes the effect produced when one sees a
movie which shows his very neighborhood. The film "certifies,"
to use Percy's term, an otherwise humdrum and familiar reality

9. *Language, Truth and Logic.* 2nd ed. (New York: Dover, 1946), p. 120.
10. *Words and Images: A Study in Theological Discourse* (London: Libra,
1968), p. 2.

and, in so doing, evokes a new "knowledge" of it.[11] The important thing to note is that the film adds no new empirical data to the scene nor does it in anyway encourage new analytical inferences. But it does cause the scene to take on a "depth" which one could claim possesses cognitive significance. Similarly, Gerard Manley Hopkins' poem "Carrion Comfort" gives us in its final lines a discernment in which the latent depth of the narrator's own description of his nocturnal struggle with God is abruptly self-"certified" in the very middle of his recollection of "That night, that year / Of now done darkness [when] I wretch lay wrestling with (my God!) my God." Again, it is a naked realization, one innocent of any new data or empirically-altered circumstances, which constitutes the cognitive yield of the situation for the anguished persona of the poem. It is an instance, I would judge, of the purest God-talk.

The thrust of this general reply to those who challenge the cognitive credentials of God-talk is simply that there do exist situations which yield genuine knowledge but which nevertheless do not rely upon empirical or analytical input. What, then, is the nature of the input to God-talk that saves it from total subjective insulation? The Christian would claim, I believe, that the very metaphors and images that his God-talk exploits are themselves revelatory by virtue of the fact that they are supported and informed by the authority of the Bible. There is a difference, in other words, between the mere "rational analogies" which secular poetry exploits for its metaphors and the "revealed images" which make up the metaphorical fund of God-talk. Unlike secular poetry, God-talk is not at liberty to employ just any apparently apt analogy from nature. To the contrary, as we shall see at the end of the next chapter, God-talk is restricted to figures which possess revelatory power through their status as the inspired vocabulary of the Word of God. "The images through which the Christian revelation is mediated to us," comments E. L. Mascall, "do not function simply in virtue of their iconic character, simply by being the sort of images they are, in such a way that they would carry their message to any human being in any age who happened to stumble upon them. Their efficacy does not depend

11. *The Moviegoer* (New York: Knopf, 1962), p. 63.

simply upon the natural power of the human mind to recognize likenesses, to abstract universals from particulars, to 'put things together and take them apart,' as Aristotle says. The images were provided by God to his ancient people the Jews in the Old Testament revelation, they were taken by Christ and refashioned and synthesized, and this work continues in the Apostles and the Church."[12]

The defense of God-talk as a cognitively significant stratum of language, then, rests, appropriately, upon the same foundation as the system of belief from which it springs: the revealed Word of God as articulated in the Bible.

Although Chapter Three will contain a fuller discussion of the dynamics of God-talk, it may be helpful to suggest a few of its more observable characteristics to place us in a better position to detect its presence and adapt to its logic. I pass over its most obvious and superficial properties, i.e., Biblical archaisms and specialized theological vocabulary, in order to emphasize that it shares the same basic vocabulary and syntax as ordinary language. It gains its structural distinction from the way in which the word "God" (or key surrogate terms) establishes complete semantic control over virtually any context in which it is placed. "God" is the semantic cornerstone of God-talk and does not take predication in the same way that other proper nouns do. Compare, for example, the statement "God created the heavens and the earth" with "Christopher Wren created St. Paul's"; or "God is on my side" with "the police commissioner is on my side"; or still again, "God loves me" with "Jenny loves me." Despite their apparent *syntactical* parallelism, these comparisons are striking examples of *logical a-symmetry*. If we replace the nouns "Christopher Wren," "the police commissioner," and "Jenny" with "God," we see immediately the qualitative change that the oddly-behaved noun inflicts on such sentences. God's creativity means something rather more to the believing Christian than does Wren's, God's sustaining support is of a fundamentally different order than the backing of one's local police commissioner, and God's love suggests a comprehensiveness and quality hardly to be expected of anyone's Jenny. The point is that the sheer presence of "God", implicitly or

12. *Words and Images*, p. 119.

explicitly felt in a linguistic context, radically changes the semantic terrain; it literally tyrannizes the structure of the discourse into which it is introduced. This phenomenon is so automatic and predictable that it can be said to precipitate a language pattern sufficiently unique to warrant isolation and classification by the term God-talk. "God," I. M. Crombie quips, "is a very improper proper name."[13]

The word "God" also creates the analogical duality which I previously mentioned as a characteristic of God-talk. The intrusion of this key concept into an otherwise neutral context has the effect of automatically creating two planes of meaning. Take, for example, a verbal context that contains the words "pasture," "water," "path," "valley," "table," "enemy," "oil," "house," and so forth. Most of us would probably recognize these as the determinative words of the 23rd Psalm. As they are arranged in that psalm they make perfect ethical and *non*-theological sense so long as we ignore the initial controlling metaphor: "The *Lord* is my shepherd." But the point is that the word "Lord," in its full theological sense, tyrannizes the context so effectively that all the other words of the psalm are wrenched into an additional theological meaning beyond that of their ordinary denotations.

God-talk can often be detected by its "open" texture. Its surface is often literally riddled with holes — gaping caesuras, lacunae, pregnant pauses and mysterious omissions. Carl Michalson has called these holes "paratactic gaps" because they witness a deficiency of connectives. Oftentimes sentences, phrases or images in God-talk "just seem placed alongside each other. There is no sign of syntax, of connectedness. They are, that is, paratactic."[14] In the Bible, for example, we find statements like: "God said, Let there be light! And there was light"; "Once I was blind. Now I see." The gaps in the middle of these assertions are repositories of religious mystery. They defy conceptual *analysis* at the same time they invite *interpretation*. They do not so much *inform* the listener as actively *engage* him and make demands upon him. *He* must supply the interpretive caulking with his discernment and his commitment. God-talk is nothing without audience participation, and

13. *Faith and Logic,* pp. 31-67.
14. *The Hinge of History* (New York: Scribner's, 1959), p. 35.

to assure participation it leaves its canvases incomplete.

In general, God-talk usually strives to baffle our conceptual habits of mind by confronting us with what Ian Ramsey calls "logical improprieties."[15] Not only does the word "God" initiate such improprieties, but supporting confusion is supplied by paradox and deliberate ambiguity. In Chapter Three we will have occasion to discuss Ramsey's provocative analysis of religious language based upon his theory of "models and qualifiers," but for the present it is enough merely to point out the subversive character of God-talk vis-a-vis the conventional conceptual patterns of logical thought. In all instances, God-talk is in the business of promoting mystery and suppressing the purely literal statement. It is an oblique and intuitively provocative language that encourages and demands of us that we accept it on its own often peculiar terms.

It should be apparent that a recognition and appreciation of the logical behavior of God-talk ought to be a *sine qua non* for Christian literary criticism. Without it, we are vulnerable to the enormously embarrassing consequences of underreading. How many times are Christian authors damned for alleged narrative failures by critics naively missing the religious point of what they have just read? In Chapter Five we will see how even a critic as sensitive to the evocative force of positive ambiguity as William Empson can be seduced by the pictorial clarity of a stanza in Herbert's "The Sacrifice" into rendering an interpretation so literal that it ridicules the otherwise moving religious conduct of the poem.

Fluency in God-talk can save us embarrassed blushes, but perhaps more importantly it can help us escape our conditioned literary *bias* toward the literature of worship, which invariably keeps us looking for the wrong things. It can help us relearn how to read such classics as *The Temple, Paradise Lost,* or *LXXX Sermons* with an equal (or greater) attention paid to their *functional* than to their aesthetic aims. How many times do we "forgive" a successful dramatist a narrative or aesthetic lapse in his pursuit of the powerfully moving scene? Here, at least, we acknowledge and respect the natural priorities of the theatre. Why can we not do the same for religion? One might legitimately inquire, for example, how we

15. *Religious Language,* p. 179.

ought to read Milton's notorious depiction of God in Book Three of *Paradise Lost.* Read literally, the grossness of the anthropomorphisms becomes clearly offensive. Read symbolically, the dramatic immediacy of the scene is lost. Read narratively, the moral and ethical behavior of God is repulsive. But what if it is read as God-talk? What if we conceived Milton's God, Heaven, Hell, Chaos and Paradise not as literal realities, nor as symbols, nor even as metaphors, but as admittedly inadequate worldly models which have been religiously qualified so as to evoke a characteristically religious response within a characteristically religious reader? Then our attention would center not upon the aesthetic or narrative success of the scene, but upon its success in evoking religious awareness. Difficult or perhaps impossible as the measurement of the latter is, it cannot be dismissed as an irrelevant interpretive concern. It is, after all, the central concern of most Christian authors.

Another advantage that fluency in God-talk can afford the critic is a means for testing the integrity of a religious work. Often the trappings of Christian piety are exploited by writers for the most impious of reasons: aesthetic laurels. An obvious fraudulence attends such writing, especially when it takes place in forms purporting to be functionally devotional. Here, the ability to detect God-talk might serve as a kind of critical litmus. It could easily distinguish Christian literature from mere literature *about* Christianity.

These are merely preliminary suggestions as to how God-talk might be useful to the literary critic, but these views are based upon certain realities about the behavior of theological utterances which more often than not seem to me to be neglected by even sensitive readers of Christian literature. What I am suggesting, in the jargon of the day, is a re-ordering of our priorities as far as the criteria for evaluating religious literature are concerned. I would like to see attention directed to the fact that in Christian literature matters of aesthetics must necessarily yield to the requirements of vocational efficiency, that is, the demands of the religious job the work is charged to perform. A glaring illustration of our insensitivity to this fact is the popularity of the term "devotional poetry." The phrase is disturbingly misleading because it places determinative emphasis upon the wrong word. "Poetic devotion" pays more honor to the reality of the enterprise.

I am a bit sensitive about a final point that I feel compelled to bring up. It would seem from a number of my comments on the priority of religious over literary vocation in Christian writing that it would make a difference whether a reader were a believer or not. It has always seemed to me that literary criticism has never seriously faced up to this question and has preferred to brush aside the matter as irrelevant. It should make no difference whether you believe in God or not when you read *Paradise Lost,* the argument runs. In fact, disbelief is probably an advantage because theological obstacles will not be as apt to get in your way. I can see the logic of this position because I myself am a religious agnostic. Nevertheless, I suspect that the reason criticism brushes aside the question of belief so cavalierly is that it threatens to embarrass traditional assumptions. Literature, for example, has always been divided into the two functional categories of teaching and pleasing, *sentence* and *solace.* How does it deal with a body of literature dedicated and organized to demand from its readers a total commitment? How does it deal with a literature that defies analysis, seemingly invites interpretation, but ultimately ends up interpreting the reader? How does it accommodate a literature that is so aggressively performatory that in its very utterance it "does something" to the reader in the same way that the bridegroom's "I do" does something to him? My fear is that literary criticism, unable to meet God-talk on its own terms, reduces it to its own more manageable principles, thereby effectively emptying it of its inherent wonder and mystery.

The believer, I contend, is not so handicapped. He knows precisely what to look for in the Christian literature before him because he is attuned to the functional intention of the author. He will naturally assume the correct priority between religion and art because it will never occur to him to do otherwise. The philosopher Geddes MacGregor supports me in this conviction when he notes that for the believer "the religious work of art has a value other than that which it has for the art connoisseur as such. We expect every cultured person to value Raphael's *Madonna,* if not El Greco's *Agony in the Garden,*" he points out, "but the religious person, as such, however cultured, does not value them very much more than most inferior works of a similar kind; for he is looking not for aesthetic experience alone, but for the initiation of a trend of experience leading towards a union with God."[16]

This leaves me and perhaps other literary critics of religious literature in a rather awkward position. Unless we are believers, it might appear, our appreciation of a religious work of art is restricted to its secondary intention — its aesthetic worth. We are blocked from fully appreciating the determinative *vocational* nature of the work, and even more important, we may be deficient in seeing important dynamic relationships between aesthetics and vocation within the work itself.

I recognize the problem, and barring the advent of a compelling religious fervor I am afraid I will have to admit to unavoidable blind spots in my appreciation of a large quantity of seventeenth-century literature. In spite of this, however, I can at least try to read this literature as if I *were* a true believer. My inquiry into the behavior of the language I call God-talk, therefore, is a small contribution to my own willing suspension of disbelief, and my only hope is that it might in some small way assist others like myself to peer as through a glass darkly into the total kind of experience which prompted and sustained men like George Herbert, John Milton and John Donne to do what they did.

16. Aesthetic Experience in Religion (London: MacMillan, 1947), p. 213.

Chapter Two: Devotion and "The Flower"

Devotion is an activity of the will. Its "central and pervasive assumptions," as Louis Martz describes them, are "that man, whether he will or not, lives in the intimate presence of God, and that his first duty in life is to cultivate an awareness of that presence." Martz goes on to say, "The aim of meditation is to apprehend the reality and the meaning of the presence of God with every faculty at man's command."[1] The very words that these descriptions find it necessary to employ — the *duty* of the believer, the *aim* of the meditation, the *cultivation* of divine awareness — bear out a simple truth which is too seldom stressed: that devotion, poetical or not, has a specific religious job to perform, that its primary *raison d'être* is vocational. I believe it is necessary to emphasize the utilitarian intent of poetic devotion to counter the efforts of those aesthetically-preoccupied readers who, in preferring the term "devotional poetry," confess to a bias which, in my opinion, encourages not only a general "under-reading" of this literature but misleading explications of it as well. Most unfortunately, by placing the literary cart before the devotional horse they forfeit an appreciation of how intimately — even organically — poetry and piety conspire to evoke religious insight.

The usual objections to poetical devotion as a genre center around the scrupulous conviction that poetry and piety have no business together. Does not poetry (because it is artifice) inevitably compromise the sincerity required by religious devotion? We may recall Dr. Johnson objecting that "contemplative piety, or the intercourse between God and the Human soul, cannot be poetical, Man admitted to implore the mercy of his Creator, and plead the merits of his Redeemer, is already in a higher state than poetry can

---

1. *The Meditative Poem: An Anthology of Seventeenth-Century Verse*, ed. Louis L. Martz (Garden City, L.I.: Anchor, 1963), p. xviii. Geddes MacGregor broadens the issue to include all religious activity: "However we interpret the term 'religion,' the ultimate goal of religion must in fact be some kind of vital union with divine being." (*Aesthetic Experience in Religion*, p. 193).

confer."[2] Or we may remember George Herbert's ubiquitous "friend" who whispers at the end of "Jordan (II)," "How wide is all this long pretence! / There is in love a sweetnesse readie penn'd: / Copie out only that, and save expense." Perhaps piety *ought* appropriately to proceed in plain dress, but considering the demands placed upon a language obligated to deal with an ineffable subject, how much plainness can even God-talk afford and still be effective? It seems to me that Johnson, at least as he expresses himself here, reveals an alarming innocence about the degree to which religious utterances *depend* upon the resources of poetry as their only alternative to silence.[3]

In order to "cultivate an awareness" of the presence of God, a poetic devotion, from all descriptions of it, is performatory, that is, it does something to the psychology of the devotee in a religiously salutary way. Presumably the poetic art of the devotion assists in this religiously-oriented process, for if it does not, if it is non-functionally ornamental, the devotional enterprise is open to charges of inefficiency and insincerity. Unfortunately the criticism of poetic devotions has not always been able to maintain a view toward the priority of devotion and poetry which is religiously rewarding. This is understandable. *Literary* critics naturally harbor *literary* biases. Under normal circumstances, they can hardly be

2. *The Life of Waller.* Johnson reasons that "the essence of poetry is invention as, by producing something unexpected, surprises and delights. The topics of devotion are few, and being few are universally known; but, few as they are, they can be made no more; they can receive no grace from novelty of sentiment, and very little from novelty of expression."

3. *"Non ut illud diceretur, sed ne taceretur"* (not because the phrases are adequate – they are only an alternative to silence), St. Augustine, *de Trin.*, v. 9. Dr. Johnson on Boehme: "If Jacob saw the unutterable, Jacob should not have tried to utter it." (Quoted by Alasdair MacIntyre, *Metaphysical Beliefs* [London: SCM, 1957], p. 178). Thomas MacPherson: "There are some things that just cannot be *said.* As long as no one tries to say them there is no trouble. But if anyone *does* try to say them he must take the consequences. We ought to try to express the inexpressible. Now the things that theologians try to say (or some of them) belong to a class of things that cannot *be* said. The way out of the worry is retreat into silence." ("Positivism and Religion," *Religious Language and the Problem of Religious Knowledge,* ed. Ronald E. Santoni [Bloomington, Indiana: Indiana University Press, 1968], p. 54).

expected to appreciate either the quality of divine awareness or the conditions required to bring it about, both concerns which would be first in the mind of the faith-oriented devotee. Instead, literary critics invariably draw back into the comfort of their "discipline" and draw up what amounts to non-religious accounts of religious activities. They usually manage to disguise their language-game-mixing even from themselves by arguing that their accounts do justice to the devotions because their "explanations" of the poems (neatly arranged in footnotes) indeed do seem to clear up "problems." Unfortunately, it is usually the "problems" that hold the elusive religious potential of most good poetical devotions, and, as they are explained away, the vocational essence of the devotion — its ability to evoke the awareness of the presence of God — evaporates before the pressure of our doggedly conceptual explications. Nothing is wrong with this procedure — "Reading a devotional poem aesthetically and putting it into practice," as Ross Garner rightly notes, "are different, not inconsistent, activities"[4] — but we should not presume that in conceptualizing the God-talk of these poems we are in any way increasing our awareness of their originally-intended depth.

The devotee, on the other hand, not valuing the poetical devotion for aesthetic experience so much as "for the initiation of a trend of experience leading towards a union with God,"[5] looks for different things in it and reads it in a different way. Rather than seeking to reduce the elements of the poems to their literal equivalents, he goes in precisely the opposite direction. Obscurities and problems, which would be serious obstacles (even threats) to a conceptual account of the poem, are for him opportunities for escape from conceptual limitations. The poetic devotion, in other words, ideally offers the devotee a chance to supplement the highly conceptualized dogma of Christianity with experiences which are personal, non-conceptual, yet nonetheless significant and of the very essence of religious faith. It serves the kind of religious thirst which caused Sir Thomas Browne to delight in losing

---

4. *The Unprofitable Servant in Henry Vaughan,* University of Nebraska Studies, 29 (Lincoln, 1963), p. 29.
5. Geddes MacGregor, *Aesthetic Experience in Religion,* p. 213.

himself in Christian mystery and pursuing his "reason to an *oh altitudo.*"[6]

The goal of the poetic devotion is neither didactic nor conceptual. Indeed, its congeniality with (even dependence upon) poetic expression suggests that its quest lies beyond the range of conventional language. But the "quest" itself remains mysteriously obscure, shrouded from secular consciousness by its claim to an "awareness of the presence of God." What does it mean to experience "the presence of God"? What sort of "meaning" can a poetic devotion claim to evoke? Finding the language devoid of a term for the unadulterated religious experience which "awareness of the presence of God" seems to warrant, the German theologian Rudolf Otto coined the word "numinous" to describe the part of religious experience that cannot be conceptualized, that is, the non-rational. A "sense of the numinous," Otto believed, is partly a feeling (specifically a feeling of dependence) and partly a consciousness of "something outside" us, something "Wholly Other." The "numinous" is a "clear overplus of meaning" which remains in the word "holy" after all denotations of *good* or even *absolute goodness* have been drained from it. The "numinous state of mind," Otto contended, "is *sui generis* and irreducible to any other; and therefore, like every absolutely primary and elementary datum, while it admits of being discussed, it cannot be stricly defined."[7]

I stress Otto's account of the numinous because I think it lends a precision to the kinds of questions one can ask of poetic devotion's vocational obligation. Granting that there is at least a rough correlation between "an awareness of the presence of God" and a "sense of the numinous," we can outline the vocational "problem" of the poetic devotion in this fashion: 1) One cannot conceptually define the "numinous" satisfactorily; 2) One cannot even tell others what it is; 3) One can, however, remind others of experiences which are like the numinous feelings; 4) One can talk analogically round and round these "like" experiences (never directly expressing the sense of the numinous because it is inex-

6. *Religio Medici*, i.9.
7. *The Idea of the Holy*, trans. John W. Harvey (Harmondsworth, Middlesex: Penguin, 1923), pp. 15-25.

pressible in words) until the reader is brought to a point where he sees for himself what the "sense of the numinous" is.[8] This latter strategy is, of course, the essence of God-talk.

Poetry is obviously ideally suited to resolving the devotional problem if for no other reason than its freedom from conceptual constraints. Poetry is accustomed to coaxing insights from readers through analogical prodding, but this does not automatically assure that if a devotion is poetical it must, therefore, be valid God-talk and potentially evocative of the numinous. The issue is: how well does a particular poetic devotion burn its conceptual bridges behind it. Does its analogical activity propel the reader toward the numinous or does it merely draw him conceptually back to each analogy's literal equivalent.

The most dismaying implication of Dr. Johnson's rejection of poetic devotion (on the grounds that piety cannot be poetical) is the assumption that metaphors are mere superfluous adornments (therefore articifial and insincere) because they are mere transformations of more reliable *literal* meanings, that any metaphorical expression is merely a "stand-in" for an equivalent literal statement. If metaphorical language is no more than this — if Johnson is right — God-talk (which stands or falls on whether or not its metaphors have cognitive significance of their own) and poetic devotion (which depends upon the validity of God-talk) are meaningless, anthropomorphic babble. Such a view of poetry and God-talk has not cut its conceptual apron strings. Its reference is always back toward the literal, never out toward the numinous.

8. Otto's own description of the process: "There is only one way to help another to an understanding of it. He must be guided and led on by consideration and discussion of the matter through the ways of his own mind, until he reach the point at which 'the numinous' in him perforce begins to stir, to start into life and into consciousness. We can cooperate in this process by bringing before his notice all that can be found in other regions of the mind, already known and familiar, to resemble, or again to afford some special contrast to, the particular experience we wish to elucidate. Then we must add: 'This *X* of ours is not precisely *this* experience, but akin to this one and the opposite of that other. Cannot you now realize for yourself what it is?' In other words our *X* cannot, strictly speaking, be taught, it can only be evoked, awakened in the mind; as everything that comes 'of the spirit' must be awakened" (*Ibid.*, p. 21).

Fortunately, there are other ways of regarding the metaphor beyond the crude formulation that it is a way of saying one thing and meaning another. Max Black, for instance, points out that the literal paraphrase of a metaphor is inevitably weak not because it "may be tiresomely prolix or boringly explicit (or deficient in qualities of style)" but because "it fails to be a translation because it fails to give the insight that the metaphor did."[9] Black himself prefers an "interaction view " of metaphor, which he describes as one having the "power to bring two separate domains into cognitive and emotional relation by using language directly appropriate to the one as a lens for seeing the other; the implications, suggestions, and supporting values entwined with the literal use of metaphorical expression enable us to see a new subject matter in a new way. The extended meanings that result, the relations between initially disparate realms created, can neither be antecedently predicted nor subsequently paraphrased in prose. We can comment *upon* the metaphor, but the metaphor itself neither needs nor invites explanation and paraphrase."[10] Here is a metaphor with a cognitive value *in itself*; it not only does not need a literal equivalent, it would lose its potential for religious insight if it had one! It is, as Black points out, a metaphor that itself can be used literally. Such metaphors deserve Ian Ramsey's description of them as "purveyors of insight,"[11] for they provide the means by which God-talk defends itself against the charge that its utterances are logical non-sense.

The vocational potency of a poetic devotion is directly proportionate to the quality of the God-talk it employs, and one practical test for determining the vocational efficiency of a devotion, derivable from this axiom, is to ascertain if the metaphorical expressions of a particular devotion "interact" or if they merely "stand in" for literal equivalents. This test is also useful for determining the religious integrity of the work, for if the devotion is not written in God-talk, can it really be said to be intended for God or should it be conceded that it has at least one eye on the hopefully appreciative ears of worldly eavesdroppers? I must

9. *Models and Metaphors* (Ithaca: Cornell University Press, 1962), p. 46.
10. *Ibid.,* p. 237.
11. *Words about God,* ed. Ian T. Ramsey (London: SCM, 1971), p. 171.

reserve speaking of one further qualification required of metaphors deserving of the status of God-talk — their Biblical authority — until the end of the chapter.

I have selected George Herbert's "The Flower" as a devotional model upon which to test my assumptions not only because
Herbert's poetry is relatively free of personal idiosyncracy and,
therefore, more apt to provide an instance of pure God-talk, but
because it is a poem whose very structure is organized about a central metaphor. Moreover, "The Flower" is a poem that concerns
itself with a potentially numinal theme: the recurring awareness of
the presence and absence of God.[12]

THE FLOWER

How fresh, O Lord, how sweet and clean
Are thy returns! ev'n as the flowers in spring;
    To which, besides their own demean,
The late-past frosts tributes of pleasure bring.
        Grief melts away
        Like snow in May
    As if there were no such cold things.

Who would have thought my shriveled heart
Could have recovered greenness? It was gone
    Quite under ground; as flowers depart
To see their mother-root, when they have blown;
        Where they together
        All the hard weather,
    Dead to the world, keep house unknown.

12. Evelyn Underhill, in her discussion of the "Consciousness of the Absolute," *Mysticism: A Study in the Nature and Development of Man's Spiritual
Consciousness,* provides an account of mystic experience which precisely
parallels the phenomenon Herbert describes in "The Flower": "Intermittent
periods of spiritual fatigue or 'aridity' — renewals of the temperamental conflicts experienced in purgation — the oncoming gloom of the Dark Night — all
these may be, and often are, experienced at intervals during the Illuminated
Life; as flashes of insight, indistinguishable from illumination, constantly
break the monotony of the Purgative Way" (12th ed. [New York: Dutton,
1930], pp. 241-42.

These are thy wonders, Lord of power,
Killing and quick'ning, bringing down to hell
    And up to heaven in an hour;
Making a chiming of a passing-bell.
      We say amiss,
        This or that is:
    Thy word is all, if we could spell.

    O that I once past changing were,
Fast in thy Paradise, where no flowers can wither!
    Many a spring I shoot up fair,
Off'ring at heav'n, growing and groaning thither:
      Nor doth my flower
      Want a spring-shower,
    My sins and I joining together.

    But while I grow in a straight line,
Still upwards bent, as if heav'n were mine own,
    Thy anger comes, and I decline:
What frost to that? what pole is not the zone,
      Where all things burn,
      When thou dost turn,
    And the least frown of thine is shown?

    And now in age I bud again,
After so many deaths I live and write;
    I once more smell the dew and rain,
And relish versing: O my only light,
      It cannot be
      That I am he
On whom thy tempests fell all night.

    These are thy wonders, Lord of love,
To make us see we are but flowers that glide:
    Which when we once can find and prove,
Thou has a garden for us, where to abide.
      Who would be more,
      Swelling through store,
    Forfeit their Paradise by their pride.

    An "aesthetic" account of the metaphorical activity in this poem might run something like this: a man's experience of the rhythmic "killing and quick'ning" of his soul (brought about by the corresponding absences and returns of God's revitalizing presence) is expressed through the medium of a perennial flower. The literal meaning of the poem, L, is translated into metaphor, M. The delight that the poem affords comes from the working out of an enjoyable puzzle. We "solve" M by tracing it back to L. In doing so, we experience what Black describes as "a shock of agreeable surprise."[13] What "happens" metaphorically in the poem becomes exhaustively explained under the pleasure principle. As aesthetes, we are pleased by the cleverness with which the poem prettifies L with a paraphraseable M. The point of "The Flower" becomes not devotion but aesthetic delight. Yet, to read "The Flower" this way and imagine that we have in any way experienced its potential religious depth is not only to reveal our illiteracy in God-talk, but to drain the poem of all but its most superficial religious traces. Such an aesthetic preoccupation at the expense of vocational concern is tantamount to inspecting with minute care and delight every frill on board the yacht we intend to purchase without bothering to inquire if it floats.

An account informed by the principles of God-talk, however, is unconcerned with playing delightful transpositional games with L and M. On the other hand, it is intensely concerned with the way L and M, as "two separate domains" of mankind and flowerdom, come together, interact, and become numinously alive. If we observe the metaphorical development of the poem, we can see how Herbert has coaxed these two domains gradually into a religiously rewarding merger. The poem opens with the lowest level of metaphorical relationship, the simile. But we notice that what begins as a mere comparison of a man re-experiencing grace and a flower re-experiencing spring (a metaphorical situation with slight numinal potential) by line nine begins to fuse into a single entity ("Who would have thought my shrivel'd heart / Could have recover'd greenness? "). The adjective "shrivel'd" and the noun "greenness" are perfect examples of how the interaction metaphor uses "language directly appropriate to the one [contextual domain] as a lens for seeing the other." These words successfully bond the elements of the simile to achieve an actual identification; the man becomes the flower, the flower the man. The simile has

13. *Models and Metaphors,* p. 32.

matured into a metaphor proper and a healthy ambiguity as to whether the flower is a "stand-in" for man, or man a "stand-in" for flower is already apparent. Moreover, the ambiguity has been encouraged by Herbert through the subtle use of a pronoun. The "shrivel'd heart", the poem tells us, has gone "underground", paralleling the departure of the flowers "To see their mother-root." The self-conscious parallelism of the two departures seems an apparent partial reversion of metaphor back to simile except for the fact that the pronoun "they" of line twelve urges us less toward the literally-satisfying antecedent, "flowers," than toward the metaphorically-satisfying antecedents, "heart" *and* "flowers" which together *share* respite from "the hard weather." If we insist that "they" refers only to "flowers" (thus maintaining the literal integrity of the simile), we become hardpressed to see the point of Herbert's going to such metaphorical pains to introduce the clever notion of subterranean housekeeping (line fourteen) if it is merely an elaboration of what itself is an elaboration of the condition of the human heart. It is an instance, characteristic of God-talk, of a poem itself resisting a literalism its own grammar seeks to impose. The poem fashions ordinary poetic language into God-talk by systematically breaking down distinctions between what is "device" and what is "real meaning." It destroys the conceptual basis of simile by effecting not an analogy but a confluence of two mutually enriching contexts on a linguistically egalitarian level.

Is there any way by means of which the nature of the experience evoked by the mutual enrichment of the man and flower contexts might be even suggested? We are asking, of course, for a conceptual account of a radically non-conceptual experience and should not expect more than an analogical prodding which conceivably might help us to experience the feeling for ourselves. Theology has always faced the challenge (particularly in the area of Apologetics) of having to translate as best it can religious feelings into conceptual dogma, and at least one Thomist exercise in that art is helpful here. St. Thomas made a distinction between analogy *unius ad alterium* (a form of analogy similar to what we have been calling a "stand-in" metaphor) and analogy *duorum ad tertium.*[14] The latter analogy might be described as

---

14. *Summa Theologica,* I, xiii, 5c; *Summa Contra Gentiles,* I, xxiv.

one that "holds between two beings in consequence of the relation that each of them holds to a third."[15] If we apply the analogy *duorum ad tertium* to the central metaphor of "The Flower," we discover that the flower and man contexts provide mutual enrichment not merely on the basis that each serves as a lens for seeing the other, but because both are co-efficiently evocative of a third context which relates them in a manner over and above their mere relations *unius ad alterium*. The metaphorical structure of "The Flower," we might say, generates a total insight much greater than the sum of its admittedly insightful parts, for the third context that is evoked is none other than an awareness of the presence of God exercising His sustaining power over all His Creation. At least part of the experience is sacramental, and it involves certainly an appreciation of divine wonder, which theology has customarily been wise to shield from all attempts at conceptualization. Herbert uses the two interacting contexts of his poem to create a stereoptic perspective potentially capable of triggering a discernment into the real subject of his poetic devotion: not flower, not man, but a sense of the numinous. To adapt language from Evelyn Underhill, Herbert's poem "ceases to be a picture, and becomes a window through which the [devotee] peers out into a spiritual universe, and apprehends to some extent — though how he knows not — the veritable presence of God."[16]

Another vocational feature of "The Flower" is that it not only expresses itself in God-talk, but it affords tutelage for the devotee to bring him to fluency in it. In a process similar to what we call "programed learning" in today's jargon, "The Flower" systematically confronts its reader with progressively more sophisticated metaphorical challenges (which, in fact, turn out to be devotional challenges as well). As we have seen, he enters the poem at the level of an apparent simile. The simile quickly ripens into metaphor. The metaphor's constituents are soon after forced into interaction, and finally, as I hope to show, the interaction metaphor leads to an escape from the conceptual altogether by precipitating the Christian paradox. Granted, at each metaphorical

15. Eric Mascall, *Existence and Analogy* (London: Longman's, 1949), p. 100.

16. *Mysticism*, p. 315.

challenge up to the paradox, the reader can opt out to the conceptual, but he does so at the cost of a potential religious discernment and commitment which, of course, the sense of the numinous involves.

Like metaphor, the paradox can be understood either conceptually or numinously. Philip Wheelwright distinguishes between "surface" and "depth" paradoxes by pointing out that the aim of the former is "to startle, amuse, and more seriously to jolt the reader or hearer into reexamining the relation between some pair of ideas that he had hitherto taken for granted."[17] The "depth" paradox, on the other hand, "expresses some transcendental truth which is so mysterious and so many-sided in its suggestions of explorative possibilities that neither half of it could be affirmed separately without gross distortion."[18] The surface paradox, like the "stand-in" metaphor, is firmly grounded in the conceptual; the "depth" paradox has the characteristic open-endedness of the utterances of God-talk.

The difference between the interaction metaphor and the depth paradox is that in the one case a *merger* of two contexts takes place and in the other a *confrontation* of contexts occurs. Before a depth paradox can become numinously affective, a commitment to a prior discernment must have taken place, for, only an attitude properly cleansed of conceptual habits is in a position to receive the paradox not as contradiction but as possibility. From metaphor to paradox there occurs the same qualitative change that characterizes the devotee's leap from reason to faith. The catalogue of God's wonders in the third stanza of "The Flower" appropriately exploits paradox in a series of three progressive challenges ending in a commitment situation of the first order:

> These are thy wonders, Lord of Power,
> Killing and quick'ning, bringing down to hell
> And up to heaven in an hour;
> Making a chiming of passing bell.

The "wonders" are expressed through three pairs of colliding

---

17. *The Burning Fountain: A Study in the Language of Symbolism*, rev. ed. (Bloomington, Indiana: Indiana University Press, 1968), p. 97.
18. *Ibid.*, p. 98.

life-death contexts, which at each stage decrease the possibility of literal equivalency. The conceptually-comprehensible "killing and quick'ning" is raised to a more difficult tropological dimension by its association with "hell" and "heaven." In turn, "hell" and "heaven" are elevated to the status of a genuine depth paradox when it is asserted that a bell which invokes life is also a death's knell. Three successive ranks of life-death contexts build to a final discernment, released through paradox, which can be conceptually hinted at by the Christian claim that to die is to be born again. No argument can be raised against the objection that even this paradox can be conceptually resolved through the simple application of Christian dogma, other than to resurrect the Reformation distinction between the natural man's reason and the "right" or "rectified" reason of the regenerate Christian, which, in fact, "The Flower" itself, as we shall see, does.

John Donne once preached the common Christian psychology of his day by pointing out that "a regenerate Christian, being now a *new Creature,* hath also *a new facultie of Reason*: and so believeth the Mysteries of Religion, out of another Reason, then as a meere natural Man, he believed naturall and morall things."[19] It is not difficult to see that this kind of isolation of religious mystery from "naturall and morall" things roughly parallels Otto's attempt to isolate the "holy" from conceptual and ethical formulations of it. The point is that "right" reason was the Reformation's way of separating the logic of God-talk from the logic of conceptual Man-talk. Specifically, the distinction hinges on what is accepted as the authority for one's "objectivity toward the Truth:"[20] the Word of God or empirical evidence. "The Flower" sets the issue perfectly in the stanza which ends:

> We say amiss
> This or that is:
> Thy word is all, if we could spell.

The first two lines of the passage show a radical disregard of the natural reason to the point of baldly asserting that all empirical

19. *The Sermons of John Donne,* ed. George R. Potter and Evelyn M. Simpson, 10 vols. (Berkeley, 1953-62), III, sermon 17, lines 407-13.
20. The phrase is T. F. Torrance's ("Faith and Philosophy," *Hibbert Journal,* XLVII [1949], 239).

assumptions made on the basis of it are automatically "amiss." The alternative mental attitude — "right" reason — is rendered in the final line, where a commitment to "The word" is recommended as the comprehensive epistemology. The qualification "if we could spell" possesses the usual range of equivalencies and potential evocation that the God-talk of "The Flower" demonstrates throughout. At the lowest literal level it offers a conceptual association with a literal "word." On a higher analogical level it forces "Thy word" into its Christian denotation, the Bible, and suggests that the ability to spell is a figure for the inner illumination required of the Christian to make the Scriptures have particular meaning for him. Finally, "Thy word" has the perfectly valid denotation: Christ. This final possibility wrenches the meaning of the line suddenly into a radically different logical configuration, for not only is the potential discernment of an absolute Christological epistemology presented, but the possibility for commitment to it as well, in the implied invitation to learn how to "spell" the "Word" (to know Christ). At stake is the devotee's authority for objectivity toward the truth, and the stanza clearly recommends that he give up his empirical reference and surrender himself to "Thy Word." In short, God-talk is more comprehensible and reliable than Man-talk.

It should be pointed out that the semantic potency of the word "word" is dependent upon the religious authority invested in it, that is, the fact that it is a "key" Biblical term which only coincidentally possesses a natural meaning as well. The same kind of religious potency could not be expected in another word or image not so theologically-charged. The point is that authentic God-talk cannot exploit just *any* natural image, for to do so is to merely develop a rational analogy with no religious discernment potential. Revealed words and images, on the other hand, of which "word" is certainly one, are, as A. M. Farrer points out, "authoritatively communicated. The stars may seem to speak of a maker, the moral sense of a lawgiver: but there is no pattern of being we simply meet, which speaks of Trinity in the Godhead or the efficacy of the Sacraments."[21] The "word of "The Flower" not only has Biblical authority of its own, but the entire line can claim a

21. *The Glass of Vision* (London: Dacre, 1948), p. 94.

Scripturally-authorized logic *independent* of the natural reason entirely; by a simple gathering of Biblical definitions of Christ we come up with *Word, alphabet* and *all*:

> I am Alpha and Omega, the beginning and the ending,
> said the Lord . . . (Rev. 1:8)
> . . . Christ *is* all, and in all. (Col. 3:11)
> And the Word was made flesh, and dwelt among us
> . . . full of grace and truth. (John 1:14)

Armed with this kind of lexicon we can see, perhaps, the powerful evocative potential of "Thy word is all, if we could spell" when it it is put forward as a *literal* assertion to a believer possessing "right" reason.

Stanza Five of "The Flower" is a troubling one in several ways. "Many a spring, I shoot up fair," says our devout flower-man, "Off'ring at heav'n, growing and groaning thither." The tension of his willful effort seems to infect even the texture of the line. The apparent devotional sincerity inspiring the act is convincing. It is even accompanied and assisted by a comely penitence:

> Nor doth my flower
> Want a spring-shower,
> My sins and I joining together.

Surely here is a poetic model of proper devotion — clear, pure, unsullied by the least taint of impropriety.

Two lines farther on the mischief occurs. The flower grows, we learn, "in a straight line, / Still upwards bent, as if heav'n were mine own" and then comes the stinging disclaimer: "Thy anger comes, and I decline." What has gone wrong? Having expected some hope of a changeless Paradise and having proceeded upon a course which, for all appearances, seems to be the most logical to achieve that hope, why should the devotee be confronted with a scandalous demonstration of God's wrath? Surely there is an impropriety here. The language even boasts a certain rectitude with its deliberate "straight line" growth which is "Still upwards bent." The pun on "bent" suggests an appropriate decorum, as if the ascending flower-soul rose in an attitude of humble prayer. There is no question that the momentum of our expectations has been deliberately stopped short by unexpected divine anger, and we are thrown back upon ourselves for an explanation.

The conventional "explanation" (probably because it is more or less conceptual and easiest to formulate) runs along the order of the following (and I do not for one minute mean to imply that Herbert did not purposely intend this reading, although I do hope to suggest that he did not mean for it to exhaust the possibilities of the stanza): the anger is not divine whim; something central to the quality of grace is at stake in this sudden setback, and it is quite clearly delineated in the words: ". . . as if heav'n were my own." Here is pride presented to us in a new way — not in the form of a treatise, a sermon, or morality play, at which we are mere spectators, but as an event that the poem causes us to experience. Along with this personal experience, moreover, comes a discernment into the depth and nature of divine grace. The tired and perhaps boring theological dogma which declares revelation, regeneration, salvation and election to be initiated through God's grace (which is a gift and cannot be earned) is enlivened by our participation in the poem's personal evocation of pride in us. In specific doctrinal terms, Herbert has created a situation which animates the claim of the *sola fide* over the tridentine doctrine of merit at the same time that it delivers an insight into the troublesome orthodoxy of divine wrath. Should God experience anger? Should man feel pride in his spiritual accomplishments?

I am not hostile at all to this interpretation as long as it does not masquerade as a God-talk account, The problem with it is that it leaps to a moral, conceptual explanation of the mystery of the *ira deorum.* It explains away the perplexing phenomenon of divine wrath by reducing it to a mere matter of crime and punishment. To be sure, this is a useful and edifying service for the poem to perform, but it precipitates no *religiously* significant discernment. According to this explication, God's anger is qualitatively no different from that of our Uncle Frank, piqued because he thinks we have become too big for our britches.

According to Otto, the Old Testament patently shows that the "Wrath of God" has no concern whatever with moral qualities." The notion of divine anger appears regularly in a variety of religious beliefs and, as Otto points out, "There is something very baffling in the way in which it 'is kindled' and manifested. It is, as has been well said, 'like a hidden force of nature', like stored up electricity, discharging itself upon anyone who comes too near. It is 'incalculable' and 'arbitrary'. Anyone who is accustomed to think of deity only by its rational attributes must see in this 'wrath' mere caprice and wilful passion."[22] God's anger is clearly a mysterious, non-conceptual phenomenon suggestive, perhaps, of Edmund Burke's views on the sublime.[23] Otto himself equates the *ira deorum* with the religious "dread" or "awe," felt by the believer, to which he gives the name *"Tremendum,"* and he illustrates something of its character by visualizing the "shudder" which occurs when the *Tremendum* "invades the mind mightily in Christian "worship." He offers as example the hymn of Ter-steegen:

> God Himself is present:
> Heart, be stilled before Him:
> Prostrate, inwardly adore Him.[24]

The reduction of this powerful religious phenomenon to a mere matter of ethics means a qualitative change of its very nature, for, as D. Z. Phillips advises us, "The 'relation' of 'God' to the concept of anger in the statement 'God is angry' is not like my relation to the concept in the statement 'He is angry' made with reference to me. We do not share the concept of divine anger with God in the way in which we share the concept of human anger with each other. One cannot respond to God's anger in the way we respond to another human being's anger. We may say that a human being's anger is justified or unjustified."[25]

The tact with which Herbert provides only the barest hint of spiritual pride in the line, "Still upwards bent, as if heav'n were mine own," saves the numinal potential of the stanza. Otto

---

22. *The Idea of the Holy,* p. 32.

23. "Whatever is fitted in any sort to excite the ideas of pain, and danger, that is to say, whatever is in any sort terrible, or is conversant about terrible objects, or operates in a manner analogous to terror, is a source of the *sublime*" (Edmund Burke, *A Philosophical Enquiry into the Origin of our Ideas of the Sublime and Beautiful,* ed. J. T. Boulton [London: Routledge and Kegan Paul, 1958], Pt. I, sect. 7).

24. *The Idea of the Holy,* pp. 31-2.

25. *The Concept of Prayer* (London: Routledge and Kegan Paul, 1965), p. 47.

himself admits that "the idea of the wrath of God in the Bible is always a synthesis, in which the original [*ira deorum* as *Tremendum*] is combined with the later meaning [*ira deorum* as a conceptual moral phenomenon] that has come to fill it in."[26] Herbert's tactic has Scriptural backing.

I mentioned several paragraphs back that the kind of images and words which God-talk characteristically exploits for provoking religious discernment are necessarily words which can claim theological status, words which carry a religious charge by virtue of their authoritative scriptural backing. Such "revealed" words have a potency above and beyond that which might accrue to them from mere rational analogy. "The Lord *is* my shepherd" gains a definite religious impact from the fact that the word "Lord" has such decided Christian credentials. The assertion, in fact, challenges its reader to commit to a specifically Christian attitude in order to evade sheer meaninglessness. In this sense, we can see the significance of A. M. Farrer's explanation that revealed words and images "are supernaturally formed, and supernaturally made intelligible to faith. Faith discerns not the images, but what the images signify: and yet we cannot discern it except *through* the images. We cannot by-pass the images to seize an imageless truth."[27] Eric Mascall presents a similar view: ". . . the images are divinely selected and divinely arranged before they are presented to us as the *objecta quibus,* through which we can apprehend the divine realities, the *objecta quae.*"[28] In short, the "revealed" vocabulary of God-talk resists, as we have been saying all along, subjugation to conceptual contexts which invariably threaten to reduce their theological to mere analogical status. Farrer notes that "revealed images are commonly just parables," by which I take him to mean that the distinctiveness of religious parabolic statement is that it neither commends nor seeks "real and causal relation between natural organisms and Christ's mystical body."[29]

What, then, can we say about the authority for the images in "The Flower?" Is Herbert's dependence upon a flower as his

26. *The Idea of the Holy,* p. 33.
27. *The Glass of Vision,* pp. 109-10.
28. *Words and Images,* p. 120.
29. *Ibid.,* p. 12.

central metaphor proof that he was really dealing in a mere rational analogy rather than God-talk? Does Herbert's flower possess sufficient theological credentials to qualify it as a "revealed" image? The issue opens some interesting points about Herbert's artistry, for "The Flower" is in at least one way a-typical of Herbert's other poetic devotions; rarely does he exploit objects of nature as he apparently does here. More characteristic is his reliance on images directly related to the Church, its ritual, and its sacred literature. presumably because he found these images more efficient and reliable as vehicles for precipitating discernment than images with no "revealed" status. The apparent anomalous status of "The Flower" in the Herbert canon ought to alert us to the probability that the status is just that — apparent. Indeed, a search for the scriptural source of "The Flower" clearly shows that the analogical relationship of flower and man is not a rational construction of Herbert's but a parabolic coupling sponsored by the Bible itself:

> Man *that is* born of a woman *is* of a few days,
> and full of trouble
> He cometh forth like a flower, and is cut down....
> For there is hope of a tree, if it be cut down,
> that it will sprout again, and that the tender
> branch thereof will not cease.
>
> Though the root thereof wax old in the earth, and
> the stock thereof die in the ground;
> *Yet* through the scent of water it will bud, and
> bring forth boughs like a plant....
> If a man die, shall he live *again*? all the days of my appointed
> time will I wait, till my change come. (Job 14)

Herbert's interest in poetically and devotionally exploiting similarities between God's dealings with men and flora was not generated by an independent seizing of a clever, rational, analogical conceit; his interest developed from ground much more hospitable to God-talk: the Bible itself.

I cannot tell if I have in any way succeeded in hinting at ways by which "The Flower," read as God-talk, is evocative of the numinous, or even if a sense of the numinous itself passes muster as a legitimate cognitive experience. A convincing "explanation" of the process of devotion, or of poetry, or especially of poetry employed for devotional purposes, I fear, would "explain away" the very nub of the God-talk issue, for it would entail the inevitably reductionist procedure of talking about one language-game as if it were subject to the rules of another. My only possible defense is to present a series of summary assertions which, admittedly, are open to conceptual attack, but which, if I can rely on any sympathy that Wisdom's parable may have generated for his similarly imprudent apologete, may stave off God-talk's "death by a thousand qualifications" long enough for it to establish more secure beachheads in succeeding chapters. My summary statements are as follows: 1) The linguistic thrust of God-talk, like much poetry, is non-conceptual; 2) The ultimate purpose of God-talk, in various degrees depending upon the specific genre in which it is used, is to precipitate an awareness of the presence of God, or, to use the terminology of Rudolf Otto, to evoke a sense of "The Numinous"; 3) The metaphors which God-talk uses do not refer analogically to empirical equivalents but precipitate mergings of otherwise separate contexts to produce an autonomous and significant cognitive yield of their own; 4) God-talk receives its ultimate cognitive authority from the revelatory power of the Biblical images that it exclusively exploits, and this is what distinguishes it in the long run from secular poetic language.

Chapter Three: Expressing the Inexpressible

How can human beings talk intelligibly about divine subject matter? How can they express the inexpressible? Responsibility for such questions must be borne by the paradox of Christianity itself, for while Christian dogma consistently maintains that God is unknowable ("For now we see through a glass darkly"), it says at the same time that God can be known. What kind of "knowing" can Christianity mean, and through what communicative means does it find currency? Previous chapters have suggested that Christian "knowledge" involves an "over-plus" of meaning, an awareness of the presence of God, a supra-rational cognition which finds expression through utterances (usually poetic in character) which do not so much inform as throw out directional suggestions. Ian Ramsay shows his understanding of the ways of religious communication when he describes Christian doctrine as "rules for significant stuttering,"[1] and reminds us of Augustine's well-known remark that when we speak of the Three Persons of the Trinity it is "not because the phrases are adequate — they are only an alternative to silence."[2]

Those who would recommend that Christianity might serve itself best through silence usually base their recommendation on the assumption that language is the captive of the physical world. Bertrand Russell's confident and complacent dismissal of the whole God-talk question is typical:

> A spoken sentence consists of a temporal series of events; a written sentence is a spatial series of bits of matter. Thus it is not surprising that language can represent the course of events in the physical world, preserving its structure in a more manageable form, and it can do this because it consists of physical events. But if there were such a world as the mystic postulates it would have a structure different from that of

---

1. *Words About God: The Philosophy of Religion,* ed. Ian T. Ramsey (London: SCM Press, 1971), p. 219.

2. *non ut illud diceretur, sed ne taceretur,* de Trin. v. 9.

language, and would therefore be incapable of being verbally described.[3]

Russell's language restricts us to a fully-insulated, empirical world — a cognitive insularity that the very logical structure of language apparently guarantees. "The logical use of language presupposes the meanings of the words it employs and presupposes them constant," Owen Barfield points out. "I think it will be found a corollary of this that the logical use of a language can never add any meaning to it. The conclusion of a syllogism is implicit already in the premises, that is, in the *meanings* of the *words* employed."[4] Philip Wheelwright has invented the term "steno-language" to describe the logical use of language that Barfield discusses. "Steno-language," Wheelwright contends, "has the cold purity that comes from adherence to rules; and ultimately there is but a single kind of logical purity, the set ideal of all logical thinking."[5] Steno-language in its purest and most pernicious form appears in Orwell's *1984* as "Newspeak," but even in its hybrid varieties it yields the picture of a linguistic prison constructed of the bricks of petrified denotation and the mortar of the syllogism. It is a "closed" and complacent linguistic world which permits the entrance of no new knowledge. It is a language environment pledged to linguistic agnosticism.

Theism's main acknowledged weapon against steno-language is the analogy. We are all too familiar with the variety of "ways" by which a knowledge of God can be analogically pursued. There is the *via negativa,* through which God is apprehended only by taking from Him all those qualities which humans attribute to Him; the *via eminentiae,* originally a method of similitudes which eventually grew into a full-fledged doctrine of analogy; the *analogia gratiae,* through which it is asserted that God miraculously

3. *Language and Reality* (London: Allen & Unwin, 1939), p. 306. Russell's use of the term "mystic" is, of course, quite imprecise and perhaps misleading. He apparently uses it to refer to anyone who holds a belief in immaterial reality.

4. "Poetic Diction and Legal Fiction," *The Importance of Language,* ed. Max Black (Englewood Cliffs, N.J.: Spectrum Book, 1962), pp. 66-7.

5. *The Burning Fountain* (Bloomington, Indiana: Indiana University Press, 1954), p. 17.

permits his divine speech to be expressed in human speech; and finally, the *analogia entis,* central to Thomist philosophy, which understands in Being an analogical passageway to divine infinitude. The competence of all or any of these methods of extricating us from our linguistic prison is still an arguable matter today, but it seems fairly clear that bare analogy cannot escape the charge that it professes to assert supernatural fact but in reality never penetrates beyond natural phenomena. This is precisely the charge A. J. Ayer levels at religious expressions in general in *Language, Truth and Logic*: "If the sentence 'God exists' entails no more than that certain types of phenomena occur in certain sequences, then to assert the existence of a God will be simply equivalent to asserting that there is the requisite regularity in nature; and no religious man would admit that this was all he intended to assert in asserting the existence of God."[6]

Ayer's positivist point of view is clear from his arbitrary limitation of all meaningful discourse to *analytic* and *synthetic* propositions. The brashness of his challenge to God-talk, in spite of its inherent errors, has had enormous effect in forcing Theology to pay closer attention to the eccentric structure within which its utterances perform. For this reason it deserves a brief hearing.

"A proposition is analytic," according to Ayer, "when its validity depends solely on the definitions of the symbols it contains, and synthetic when its validity is determined by the facts of experience."[7] From his definitions we can see that analytic propositions were to be verified by their reducibility to tautology, and synthetic by their consistency with empirical fact. The Verification Principle, which emerged from the positivists' desire to cleanse logical discourse of all "non-sense," cleansed it as well of religion. It placed God-talk at bay.

Ayer's original assumptions about language were arbitrary enough to assure that the Verification Principle would never pose a lasting threat to God-talk. Positivism narrowly conceived the function of language as merely to inform, thereby ruling out interrogations, imperatives, performatory language and, of course, God-talk. Wittgenstein's broadside against steno-language (his in-

6. 2nd ed. (London: Victor Gollancz, 1946), p. 115.
7. *Ibid.,* p. 62.

sistence that the meanings of words are determined by their use) severely challenged the rigidity of the Verification Principle, but the most telling critique was that which hoisted the principle by its own petard: ". . . an embarrassing example of an assertion which is not meaningful when tested by the verification principle — is the verification principle itself! "[8]

The "ghost of logical positivism"[9] still lingers in many of our literary assumptions about religious writing and persistently provokes embarrassing misinterpretations which a sophistication in God-talk would automatically prevent. The challenge of the Verification Principle at least alerted Theology to the distinctiveness of its own expressions. It should also alert other disciplines to the hazards of a monolithic view of language. "To take one kind of language — call it 'logical' language — and define it by reference to analytical and synthetic propositions, this is reasonable," says David Crystal, "but to use it as an arbitrary measuring-rod for other kinds of language, condemning them for not fitting its mold, is highly unreasonable. If theological language . . . does not fit the patterns of non-theological or . . . logical positivist language, this then does not validate a dismissal of the former as being 'of unsound mind.' "[10]

God-talk can be read as steno-language only at the consequence of its virtual emasculation, but the distinctiveness of God-talk does not reside merely in its semantic behavior; it exists in its texture and tone as well. Erich Auerbach's distinction between the styles of the Homeric epic and the Bible, which he makes in *Mimesis,* is particularly interesting because it provides objective, descriptive support for the proposition that God-talk possesses a clear-cut stylistic distinctiveness that is physically observable. Epic style, according to Auerbach, is structurally different from the language found in the Bible because it possesses "fully externalized description, uniform illumination, uninterrupted connection, free expression, all events in the foreground, displaying unmistakable meanings, few elements of historical development and of psychological

8. Frederick Ferré, *Language, Logic and God* (London: Eyre and Spottiswoode, 1962), p. 53.

9. "The Ghost of Logical Positivism," *The Christian Scholar,* XLIII,226.

10. *Linguistics, Language and Religion* (New York, 1965), p. 173.

perspective."[11] Furthermore, "the separate elements of a phenomenon are most clearly placed in relation to one another; a large number of conjunctions, adverbs, particles, and other syntactical tools, . . . a continuous rhythmic procession of phenomena passes by, and never is there a form left fragmentary or half-illuminated, never a lacuna, never a gap, never a glimpse of unplumbed depths."[12]

Biblical style, on the other hand, follows a decidedly different pattern:

> . . . certain parts brought into high relief, others left obscure, abruptness, suggestive influence of the unexpressed, 'background' quality, multiplicity of meanings and the need for interpretation, universal-historical claims, development of the concept of the historically becoming, and preoccupation with the problematic.[13]

In Biblical language, Auerbach discovers, only the important points of the narrative are emphasized;

> what lies between is non-existent; time and place are undefined and call for interpretation; thoughts and feeling remain unexpressed, are only suggested by silence and the fragmentary speeches; the whole, permeated with the most unrelieved suspense and directed toward a single goal . . . remains mysterious and 'fraught with background.'[14]

Two quite disparate representations of reality are exemplified by these styles. Homer's world is horizontal in its orientation; it boasts a rigid, causal infrastructure. Little that was not intended by the author can filter through the tightly-caulked grammatical surface. There are no holes, no gaps in the texture of the epic — everything is filled by connectives. The world which Homer's language creates is a world very similar in principle to the one implied by Barfield, described by Russell and linguistically exploited by Ayer. It is self-contained and hermetically-sealed with syllogisms and verified analytic and synthetic propositions. It is the sort of "closed" laboratory world a scientist might covet as an ideal, if we can assume, as Susan Stebbing does, that "his aim is to use his

---

11. *Mimesis: The Representation of Reality in Western Literature,* trans. Willard Trask (Princeton: Princeton University Press, 1953), p. 19.

12. *Ibid.,* p. 4.

13. *Ibid.,* p. 19.

14. *Ibid.,* p. 9.

verbal symbols so as to achieve uniqueness of reference, and thus to use language in order to communicate information that is exact and precise."[15]

These comments are not intended as a criticism of Homer's style. Quite the opposite! Homer's world does not require an implied "more," a sense of background mystery or a religious depth-dimension. Homer's world is completely "in the fore-ground" and his language is entirely functional for the purpose of describing that world. (In later chapters I shall return to this matter in relation to *Paradise Lost* in which not quite the same conditions hold.) Clearly, such an informatively precise linguistic world as Homer gives us is inevitably hostile to the intuitive sug-gestiveness which God-talk strives to deliver. It is too literal a world, and Auerbach shows us how the Biblical style combats that literalism by permitting an almost infinite variety of external intrusions through its porous exterior.

There is, then, what we can at least provisionally call an "open" texture to God-talk which, Auerbach claims, also confirms its historical authority. Life, after all, can never be expected to exhibit the completeness nor the perfection of artifice. The "openness" of the Bible's style, however, not only testifies to the unfinished quality of historical writing, but also draws the necessi-ty for interpretation. That Biblical style is "mysterious," "frag-mentary," and suggestive of the "unexpressed," while epic lan-guage appears conversely to be characterized by explicitness, testi-fies to Auerbach's assertion that "Homer can be analyzed but not interpreted."[16] The fact that the Bible not only *can* be interpre-ted but *requires* interpretation suggests the different functional strategy it follows. We might say that the Homeric epic is governed by a horizontal network of logical authority; the Bible, a vertical one. Where the one finds coherence in the mutual interrelation-ships of its internal constituents, the other finds its coherence through reference to God.

Auerbach effectively describes for us how Scriptural God–talk creates a religious depth-dimension through its exploitation of

15. *A Modern Introduction to Logic,* 6th ed. (London: Methuen, 1948), pp. 16-17.
16. Auerbach, p. 11.

discernible textural idiosyncrasies, but assuming that a devotional poet has a more intimate grasp of the subtleties of religious expression than mere imitation of the Scriptures might afford him, how might he address himself to the problem of structuring his language to hurdle the phenomenal barrier that separates him from his God? John Macquarrie suggests two approaches to the problem:

> One could begin from the side of human language in its ordinary, intelligible usages, and would inquire whether and how this language can be legitimately stretched so that one can use it to talk about God . . . . The second line of approach would begin by positing the reality of God, and would then bear in mind that if we do concede God's reality, then we must think of him as coming before everything else and as making possible everything else, including any knowledge of him and talk about him. So the inquiry would begin from God, and would ask what conditions would have to be fulfilled if the divine reality is to fall, at least to some extent, within the scope of human language.[17]

Macquarrie seems to be offering inductive and deductive options. In the first case we begin with the language fund available and "stretch" it to include, if possible, meaningful discourse about God. In the second case, we deduce a logic beholden to the posited reality of God, committing ourselves to a radically theocentric language structure. Both of these approaches have compelling plausibility in relation to poetic devotion. The simplicity of most devotions, coupled with their meditative practice of initially concentrating upon empirical objects, certainly suggests the inductive pattern of beginning with the homely and familiar and building toward the divine. What Macquarrie means by "stretching" language, however, is unfortunately vague. Considering the claim of logic upon conventional discourse, it would be difficult to conceive any "stretching" process which would admit knowledge not already available to the language fund as is. The first option seems to leave us no better off than we were with analogy. The reality beyond phenomena remains unpenetrated.

Macquarrie's second option seems more in keeping with the quiet acceptance which normally characterizes the devotional poet (particularly Herbert). It sponsors a devotionally-healthy

17. *God-talk* (London: SCM Press, 1967), pp. 33-34.

climate in which philosophy and art are kept under the supervision of faith. Another way of stating this would be to say that Macquarrie's second line of approach recommends a logic of obedience according to which impartial "objectivity" does not mean subservience to "fact" but subservience to God's revealed will. No one expresses this more clearly than George Herbert in "The Flower":

> We say amiss
> This or that is;
> Thy word is all, if we could spell.

Here is a definite commitment to a theologically deductive epistemology which demands a linguistic acquiescence before God — a logical docetism — in which human values and abilities are deliberately subordinated (even obliterated) to a higher wisdom. Many may see this as humanistically repellent. Frederick Ferré bluntly characterizes it as a position in which "the 'human' is not 'inspired' but assaulted and replaced."[18]

Before concluding that poetic devotions are inevitably governed by a logic of obedience, however, we should recall from our examination of "The Flower" that such a logic of obedience really does not make itself felt until midway through that poem, after the reader has had the opportunity to adapt psychologically to the poem's will and to respond appropriately to it. In other words, the vocational strategy of "The Flower" and other devotions like it is to lead the devotee to a logic of obedience. The poem cannot *begin* on the basis of an awareness it hopes to precipitate. A keen eye toward the vocational obligation of poetic devotions makes it quite apparent that such activities cannot be *totally* dictated by theologically-deductive logical patterns. Such devotions must go both ways: human to divine and divine to human. Rosemund Tuve, for example, after noting that Herbert's "The Sacrifice" is built on a series of religiously illuminating contrasts, specifically emphasizes that they are "contrasts between man's actions towards God and God's actions towards man." She goes on to add that "the most important type is the related but profounder irony of man's wild misreading of the relation between the Creator and the creature, a relation unseen by arrogant doers

18. Ferré, p. 89.

of the actions but seen by their Sufferer in all its implications."[19]
A poet who works with such irony for devotional purposes clearly
must have double vision; his mind must be attuned to the logic of
obedience at the same time that it is sensitive to man's obdurate
commitment to "natural" logic.

Neither of Macquarrie's lines of approach by itself seems an
adequate account of how God-talk manages to pierce beyond
phenomenal limits. Macquarrie himself admits this: "Whether we
set out from human language with the intention of talking about
God, or whether we set out from the reality of God in order to
discover how he can be expressed in human language, we might
come to an impassable gulf."[20] What is required is an account of
religious language which truly satisfies both divine and human
requirements — one, that is, which has one foot firmly anchored in
empirical reality and the other poised for religious disclosure. Such
a precarious linguistic posture characterizes God-talk admirably,
particularly God-talk as it is understood by Ian Ramsey and Max
Black.[21]

I should quickly point out that neither Ramsey nor Black
are mystics nor do their claims for religious language in any way
seek to avoid the "leap" of faith. The virtue of the position they
develop, particularly Ramsey's account of it, is that it permits talk
of religious experience which evades pure subjectivity at the same
time it avoids crude anthropomorphism.. Ramsey's view of religious language is so central to my conception of God-talk and so
fertile a perspective for the literary analysis of religious texts that
it deserves a full discussion here.

Ramsey believes, along with the eighteenth-century Christian apologete Joseph Butler, that it is "contrary to experience" to
suppose that "gross bodies" are ourselves. Ramsey thus begins
with the premise that "we are more than our public behavior" or,
to put it another way, that our self-awareness is more than our

19. *A Reading of George Herbert*
20. *God-talk*, p. 34.
21. The essential positions of these two men are to be found in Ramsey's
Religious Language (New York: Macmillan, 1963) and Black's *Models and
Metaphors* (Ithaca, N.Y.: Cornell University Press, 1962). Ramsey cites his
particular indebtedness to Max Black in *Models and Mystery* (London: Oxford University Press, 1964).

body awareness. This premise, which he sees as an absolute prerequisite to religious awareness, is simply the recognition that there exist situations in life "which are perceptual with a difference, perceptual and more."[22] What we see, Ramsey is eager to convince us, does not always exhaust the meaning of the observables before us. The whole often turns out to be greater than the sum of its visible parts; as every poet and religionist is aware there is a "depth" to situations for which brute facts seldom adequately account. In other words, Ramsey agrees with Rudolf Otto's conviction that situations, particularly religious ones, carry an "overplus" of meaning, a "sense of the Numinous," which affects us independently of empirical relevance.

He provides support for his position through examples. There is the shock of recognition in an otherwise impersonal law court when the defendant faces the judge and recognizes him as her long lost husband. "Penny," she cries in shocked astonishment, calling him by his old nickname, and "an impersonal situation has come alive." A party begins "all stiff and formal. Then, it happens that someone's dinner jacket splits unexpectedly up the back; or someone sits sedately on a chair which collapses beneath her. At once the party takes on 'human warmth'; . . . 'the ice breaks.' Some theologians who were present might say the party had now entered a 'new dimension.' "[23]

Ramsey notes that the significance of the contextually odd word "Penny" and the similarly odd symbols of the torn jacket and the broken chair is "proportionate to their comparative lack of empirical relevance." He concludes that in each instance "the situation is more than 'what's seen,' it has taken on 'depth'; there is something akin to religious 'insight,' 'discernment,' 'vision.' "[24] Most important to Ramsey in these illustrations is that they all exhibit "an *objective* reference and are, as all situation, *subject-object* in structure. When situations 'come alive,' or the 'ice breaks,' there is objective 'depth' in these situations along with and alongside any subjective changes."[25] This "objective depth" is

22. *Religious Language,* pp. 15, 42.
23. *Ibid.,* pp. 21-2.
24. *Ibid.,* p. 22.
25. *Ibid.,* p. 30.

the "empirical anchorage" which Ramsey claims theological experiences possess, and it forms the means by which God-talk can be said to negotiate significantly between divine and natural reality.

Ramsey's account of God-talk as an empirically-anchored, yet religiously insightful, language system finds a practical vocabulary and a methodology through what he calls "models" and "qualifiers."[26] To illustrate what he means Ramsey addresses himself to several typical theological phrases: "First Cause," "Infinitely Wise," "Infinitely Good," "Creation *ex nihilo*" and "Eternal Purpose." He is interested to show how in each phrase an absolute empirical concept becomes stricken with logical impropriety when it is yoked to an "odd" religious qualifier. "Creation," for example, is a perfectly straightforward *empirical* notion. It has no inherent religious significance by itself. But what happens when this noun is religiously "modeled" by association with the curious qualification *"ex nihilo"*? Suddenly "Creation" is wrenched into a new dimension, one in which causal explanations are deliberately nullified in order that a new explanatory context might recommend itself. As Ramsey puts it, " 'Creation' *ex nihilo* is on the face of it a scandal: and the point of the scandal is to insist that when the phrase has been given its appropriate empirical anchorage, any label, suited to that situation, must have a logical behaviour which, from the standpoint of down-to-earth 'creation' language, is odd."[27]

God-talk, at this fundamental level, consciously develops and nurtures logical bafflements and inconsistencies which provide the basis, if I understand Ramsey correctly, for a technique of meditation. The devotee initially meditates upon "creation," imagining the varieties of creation ideas within his experience: building, painting, composing, birth and so forth. The qualifier *"ex nihilo"* serves the function of providing a specific religious direction to his meditation. "Creation from nothing" challenges his conceptual logic. He is inspired to develop "creation stories" in his mind, which strive to accommodate *ex nihilo,* until, eventually, at some point in the meditation, a qualitative changes occurs — the "penny drops," to use Ramsey's expression, the "light dawns" and he "sees" the religious insight that the phrase all along has been

26. *Ibid.,* pp. 55-102.
27. *Ibid.,* pp. 80-85.

attempting to evoke.

By way of summary, Ramsey declares that "the central problem of theology is how to use, how to qualify, observational language so as to be suitable currency for what in part exceeds it."[28] God-talk must be object language *and more*. It must be object language "which exhibits logical peculiarities, logical impropriety."[29]

Taking all things into account, how does Ramsey's account of religious language in terms of Models and Qualifiers represent an improvement over the options for religious articulation that Macquarrie cited? It does so, I think, by combining them. When Ramsey talks about "logical impropriety" as the very essence of religious language, he seems to be suggesting that idiosyncratic usage is a method of "stretching" language to do more that it normally was designed to do — a case of working from the human to the divine. But Ramsey's particular "stretching" of the language is not so extensive as to deserve calling it a linguistic "kidnap." The accommodation of God to human language can at best be mere analogical talk; at worst, grotesque anthropomorphism. Ramsey "stretches" language in order to create certain kinds of situations which provide the right kinds of settings for divine insight to enter. No claim is made that the language itself deals directly with the Ineffable. Quite to the contrary, Ramsey's God-talk is firmly rooted in the empirical, and this is what makes it different from Macquarrie's second line of approach, the language of obedience. It is not a language inspired by God to the point where human contribution counts for nothing; rather, it is a language structured in such a way that certain inhibiting forms of logic, with their concomitant literalisms, are parried and turned aside so as to permit "situations" which are distinctly open to religious disclosures of a decidedly non-conceptual sort. God-talk creates the conditions for revelation.

God-talk, perhaps like religious faith, is as much an attitude as a system of discourse beholden to rules. Nevertheless, I think it might be helpful to conclude this chapter with three guidelines for

28. *Ibid.*, p. 42.
29. *Ibid.*

those who seek an honest understanding of the literature of worship.

1. *Do not regard religious texts as other than what they are.* Poetic devotion is not identical to love poetry; a Christian epic is not the same kind of enterprise as a novel or, for that matter, a classical epic; nor is a sermon similar to a classical oration. Religious works possess a utilitarian charge. They are acts of worship *before* they are acts of art, and this fact makes itself felt down to the very formal structure of the language. "Where prayer . . . is poetry," writes Walter Kaufmann, "it is clearly not 'mere' poetry. It has religious significance only insofar as it is not contemplated aesthetically with aloof interpretation. It is poetry in which man involves himself with all his heart, soul, and power."[30]

2. *Do not confuse religious models with the reality to which they point.* Religious models, which can be situations as well as things, are never absolute in themselves. They are merely aids — directional signposts — which provide only the barest hints of the reality they seek to evoke. To speak of God as "king," "judge," "lord," or "lover" is at best to suggest a human context which might help to trigger an awareness of one small facet of the divine personality. More importantly, moral situations, appearing within a religious context, more often than not turn out to be religious models (attempts to figuratively suggest divine-human relationships) rather than absolute moral dilemmas in themselves. Often we read religiously-modeled, ethical situations as though they were mere problems in human behavior and disastrously distort their intent. We must read religious literature with a keen sensitivity to the variety of religious qualifiers embedded in it so that we do not allow ourselves to compromise the "model status" of the figures this literature exploits.

3. *Respect "logical impropriety."* Confusion, disconnectedness, ambiguity, fragmentation are anathema to steno-language but the very essence of God-talk. Rather than "explaining away" the apparent anomalies of Christian literature, we should yield to their potentialities for religious evocation. They are not liabilities but assets, the chinks through which religious insight can penetrate into our otherwise "closed" linguistic world.

30. *Critique of Religion and Philosophy* (New York: Anchor, 1961), p. 368.

Chapter Four: Herbert's Poetic God-talk

George Herbert's "Prayer (I)" provides ample confirmation of Ramsey's notion about the structure of God-talk and gives specific support for his scheme of Models and Qualifiers. The job of this poem is to evoke a sense of what it means to talk to God. An ordinary didactic explanation of prayer would never capture the "depth" of the experience which Herbert wishes to convey to his readers and, undoubtedly, himself. There is no question that the language he uses will have to be "stretched" to deal with the requirement of evoking the "something more" which distinguishes prayer from other kinds of discourse. To do this Herbert simply employs a series of qualified models in hopes that they will trigger the mind to begin movement in the right direction until the "light will dawn," "the ice will break," and a disclosure will occur:

Prayer (I)

Prayer the Churches banquet, Angels age,
Gods breath in man returning to his birth,
The soul in paraphrase, heart in pilgrimage,
The Christian plummet sounding heav'n and earth;

Engine against th'Almightie, sinners towre,
Reversed thunder, Christ-side-piercing spear,
The six-daies world transposing in an houre,
A kinde of tune which all things hear and fear;

Softnesse, and peace, and joy, and love and blisse,
Exalted Manna, gladnesse of the best
Heaven in ordinarie, man well drest
The milkie way, the bird of Paradise,
Church-bells beyond the starres heard, the souls blood,
The land of spices; something understood.

The poem is full of oxymoronic scandals and logical bafflements, but some of the most distinctive phrases are deliberately and unusually odd. "Angels age," for example, or "Gods breath in man" represent logical improprieties of the first order. "Age" is clear enough, but what happens when the qualifier "Angels" is added? A finite model is penetrated by an infinite qualifier. What is the relationship between "angels age" and the word with which it is in apposition, "Prayer"? Similarly, human breath contains no particular mystery, but what about "Gods breath in man"? Clearly something more than human respiration is at stake. Again, how does "Gods breath in man" relate to "Prayer"? The strangeness of the language does more than merely suffuse the poem with mystery; it adds a religious third-dimension. Each one of these model-qualifier pairings represents a linguistic incarnation, so to speak; a divine concept takes on empirical flesh in order to promote the kind of "depth" which eventually develops into religious discernment. What could be a better description of the process than Herbert's own phrase in the third stanza: "Heaven in ordinarie"? The "ordinary" model charged with the "Heavenly" qualifier produces potent language indeed, particularly when it is paradigmatically supported by the central act of Christianity — the Incarnation.

It is not always an adjective which causes words to be appropriately qualified. Many times the qualification takes a more subtle turn. In some cases the mere placement of a key theological word in a particularly literary context will produce the desired qualification. We will observe poems later in which a thoroughly moral body of a text is stung into religious significance merely by the almost gratuitous addition of the word "God." In any case, the pattern of God-talk invariably involves conventional expressions which are challenged by the key word "God" or its surrogate. The result inevitably is the evocation of a sense of "something more" than what is seen, a disclosure of depth. The text becomes "fraught with background."

Many of Herbert's poetic devotions exhibit what we might call inchoate forms of religious qualification, that is, cases where the intrusions of the qualifying ingredient is elemental, even experimental. We might classify these efforts as the first steps toward the more significant discernment techniques that I will discuss later. In general, these poems attempt little more than the minimum in terms of the potentialities of God-talk. They concentrate, for the most part, on evoking an *objective* depth within the situations they create, and whatever subjective, psychological effects may result are fortuitous. Their kinship with Gestalt psychology may be evident.

"Coloss. 3.3 Our Life is hid with Christ in God" is an apt, however crude, illustration of the objective deepening suggested above:

> MY words and thoughts do both express this notion.
> That LIFE hath with the sun a double motion.
> The first IS starlight, and our diurnal friend;
> The other HID, and doth obliquely bend.
> One life is wrapt IN flesh, and tends to earth:
> The other winds towards HIM, whose happy birth
> Taught me to live here so, THAT still one eye
> Should aim and shoot at that which IS on high;
> Quitting with daily labour all MY pleasure,
> To gain at harvest an eternal TREASURE.

The poem's "hidden" scriptural text opens it to charges of gimmickry, but an objective depth of a kind is nonetheless produced. The supplementary visual discernment of the hidden text, with its corresponding relevance to the title, operates in the manner of an optical illusion. A transparent cube drawn on a flat sheet of paper, for example, offers a similar flash of "depth" as the eye is suddenly tricked from a two to a three-dimensional response.

A case along these lines could also be made for "The Altar" and "Easter Wings," but more interesting are the anagrammatical devices of which Herbert is so fond. "JESU" depends upon the elementary discernment which results from phonetically pronouncing the letters in Christ's name in order to arrive, once again, at a "hidden" message: *"I ease you."*

> ### JESU
> Jesus is in my heart, his sacred name
> Is deeply carved there: but the other week
> A great affliction broke the little frame,
> E'en all to pieces; which I went to seek:
> And first I found the corner where was J,
> After, where ES, and next where U was graved.
> When I had got these parcels, instantly
> I sat me down to spell them, and perceived
> That to my broken heart he was *I ease you*
> And to my whole is JESU.

Undoubtedly this poem is organized about what Mary Ellen
Rickey calls a "serious pun" and would qualify for inclusion under
her rubric of "Sacred Quibbles."[1] The more sophisticated poem,
"Ana-Mary-gram," however, as Rosemund Tuve's explication
abundantly shows, hardly sustains the description "quibble," no
matter what the qualification, because of the extraordinary evocative richness it manages to pack into its two lines:

> How well her name an *Army* doth present
> In whom the Lord of Hosts did pitch his tent!

As Miss Tuve points out, "It would not be easy for even an ill-read
seventeenth-century Anglican cleric to avoid thinking of Mary and
Army as belonging together, and, moreover, to think of that Army
as 'The Church Militant' *as well as* Mary," but it is clear that Herbert's deliberate blending of two contexts involves more than a
mere association of ideas; the anagram effectively operates as an
interaction metaphor rising to cognitive significance of its own. As
Miss Tuve herself challenges: "I wish I knew how many of my
readers had caught on first reading the whole new spread of meaning which this double operation of the metaphor gives to a poem
that is not so tiny after all — Herbert is constantly preoccupied
with how the Lord of Hosts has 'pitched his tent' in the hearts of
his *familia,* and Mary is the great allegory of that descent and
union. The last line is not only, in other words, a reference to the
event of the Incarnation, but to the Incarnation itself as a great
metaphor."[2] The startling para-rational connections of Army and
Mary, which defy even Miss Tuve's conceptualizing skills, can, of
course, be put down as another example of an audacious metaphysical conceit, but the device itself is not as fortuitous as that
explanation would imply. Through the anagram, Herbert has
managed to release the evocative potency of God-talk. The theological status of "Mary" stings all its environment into theological
significance.

The traditional hieroglyph, as Joseph Summers' discussion
of it bears out,[3] lends itself well to the evocation of striking dis-

1. *Utmost Art: Complexity in the Verse of George Herbert* (Lexington,
Ky.: University of Kentucky Press, 1966), p. 59.
2. *A Reading of George Herbert* (London, 1952), p. 139.
3. See *George Herbert, His Religion and Art* (London: Chatto & Windus,
1954), pp. 123-46.

cernments. As is most often the case, the independent visual reaction that these poems provoke causes unexpected depth dimensions. The typographical pruning which Herbert engineers in "Paradise" translates into ethical, ecological and theological counsel, not to mention the uniquely religious insights it potentially can evoke in believers. Pruning, as a necessary procedure for encouraging fruit, is raised to God-talk status by theological qualification:

> When thou dost greater judgements SPARE
> And with thy knife but prune and PARE
> Ev'n fruitfull trees more fruitfull ARE

Like "The Flower," "Paradise" invites the reader into a vivid participation in the ecology of grace. The intent of the puns, anagrams, hieroglyphs and, in some cases, "gimmicks" is to draw attention to the personal meaning which waits for release in each of the poems. They should not be judged primarily on aesthetic decorum, but on whether or not they evoke in their readers a religiously authentic experience. Do they yield a "depth," a "something more," a "sense of the numinous" (however slight)? Do they possess what Carl Michalson calls an "invocational quality"[4] by which I take him to mean: does the poem, as opposed to a document, become an event in which the reader is decisively involved? Is he invited, even obliged, to supply filler for the gaps in the open texture of the poem's language?

Granted, the examples of hieroglyphic and pattern poetry, which we have so far cited, are rather casual, even rudimentary, attempts to evoke the type of participating discernment suggested above. Other poems by Herbert perform more subtly as indicators rather than informants, that is, they point the way toward discernment instead of attempting to provide information.

One of the most efficient "indicators" is a name. Human history has always attached a mysterious significance to names. Ernst Cassirer, for example, observes that "even a person's ego, his very self and personality, is indissolubly linked, in mythic thinking, with his name."[5] The Judeo-Christian tradition has particularly attended the magical properties of names. Genesis 2:19

---

4. *The Rationality of Faith* (New York: Scribners, 1963), p. 101.
5. *Language and Myth* (New York: Harper & Brothers, 1946), pp. 49-50.

reminds us that naming was part of the creation of the world. John 1:3 teaches that the Creation took place by the Word. God revealed himself to Moses by his name (Exodus 3:14), and among the Jews the name of God was regarded with such reverence that it was never pronounced. Macquarrie points out that "in the New Testament, it appears that the name of Jesus soon acquired a power and virtue of its own."[6] I will pay particular attention later to the disclosure of God's name in Exodus. It suffices for the present to appreciate that the discovery or the utterance of a person's name usually produces the type of depth dimension such as Ian Ramsey describes in his courtroom hypothesis. Indeed, Ramsey claims that "the word which names a person belongs . . . to a disclosure situation, to a situation which has religious significance. . . . For someone to tell us his name may be, and in a full sense always is to be, bound up with him in a characteristic religious situation."[7]

How much more religious and discerning is a situation in which God's name is uttered and the significance of the utterance itself is meditated upon? "Affliction (III)" gives us just such an example and virtually expresses, with Herbert's usual economy, what has rather laboriously been attempted in the last paragraph:

> My heart did heave, and there came forth *O God*!
> By that I knew that thou was in the grief,
> To guide and govern it to my relief,
> Making a scepter of the rod:
> Hadst thou not had thy part
> Sure the unruly sigh had broke my heart

Herbert calls the utterance *"O God"* an "unruly sigh" and it certainly was intended as an expression to signify an emotional limit-situation. In fact, the logic of the poem depends upon our understanding that the sigh occurs involuntarily (because it is "unruly") and is prompted by the extremity of grief. This sighing, in short, is parallel in principle to swearing. It is a verbal reflex which localizes a grief-stricken man's last court of appeal — God. No other word but "God" could possibly fulfill the logical requirements of this poem because the very structure of the language is geared to pro-

6. *God-talk* (London: SCM Press, 1967), p. 92.
7. *Religious Language* (New York: MacMillan, 1957), p. 125.

duce a unique *religious* disclosure. For example, it could not be claimed, as is so often of many of Herbert's poems, that this is a love poem cleverly converted to a poetic devotion simply by supplanting the "Cruel Fair" by the Deity.[8] "Helen" or "Jenny" in place of "God" reduces the poem to gibberish simply because the discernment name "God" compels the poem to operate according to certain well-defined patterns. To sigh "Helen" in the throes of lovesickness only increases the fever, but Herbert's *"O God! "* is a balm. This is very disclosure that the poem's structure is designed to evoke: God uses evil for good (the curse becomes a comfort); God's grace never ceases, even in grief; the justice and mercy of God are one, and so on. The utterance *"O God"* is a cosmic protest which paradoxically turns out to be a doorway to the discovery of a new dimension in God's dealings with men.

Having identified "God" as a key word in this poem, a word which maintains a structural control over the behavior of our response to the poem, we have broadened our concern from the mere phenomenon of discernment (which is within the power of secular poetry to create) to the special kind of *religious* discernment which carries with it the potentiality of evoking commitment as well. In "Affliction (III)" it is possible to detect in the poet's *"O God! "* a crisis which punctuates the limit of human will and, at the same time, marks the entry of Grace into the experience. What is important about this momentary tangency of human and divine wills is that we can sense the vivid identification taking place between the two concepts "I" and "God" which is emphasized in stanza two:

> But since thy breath gave me both life and shape,
> Thou knowst my tallies; and when there's assign'd
> So much breath to a sigh, what's then behinde?

The breath of the Creator is the breath of the sigh, and the enormity of the sigh bears evidence to the enormity of the grace *be-*

---

8. Louis Martz, for example, notes that "Southwell's campaign to convert the poetry of profane love had, it seems, a strong impact upon the seventeenth century," and expresses surprise that "Herbert's use of the devices and situations of popular love-poetry has not been more strongly stressed in recent criticism of Herbert" (*The Poetry of Meditation*, rev. ed. [New Haven: Yale University Press, 1962], pp. 184, 186).

hind the sigh. At the same time, the sigh has a mundane, personal significance which is in itself moving: it is a human being's expression of very real agony.

The sigh, therefore, finds its home in two worlds of experience; it spans the barrier between human and divine. There is a structural parallel between "I" and "God" which would seem to support Ramsey's contention that " 'I' will never cease to be a useful guide for us when we are confronted with puzzles about 'God',"[9] and perhaps Rudolph Bultmann's assertion that "the question of God and the question of myself are identical,"[10] as well.

I ought quickly to insist that it is not my intention here to assume an actual equation between "God" and "I," or even a metaphorical relationship. I claim only a parallelism for the purpose of demonstrating that "I" and "God" are structurally similar only in the sense that they are both bases for "significant tautologies" or perhaps more precisely "ultimates of explanation."[11] The persona in "Affliction (III)" presents his ultimate explanation of his circumstances, even his being, with the utterance *"O God!* " We can imagine, if we care to, this *"O God!* " coming as the end of a long chain of subsidiary explanations for some deep-seated malaise: sorrow, fatigue, sickness, sense of sin, and then, finally, the ultimate explanation which attempts to express that which is beyond explanation, *"O God!* " *"O God!* " in this context, is logically parallel to "I did it because I am I." Both expressions reveal a commitment of one's entire personality. One loves his beloved, for·example, ultimately because he is he, and she is she. When pressed for an explanation for his devotion to a particular girl, the lover, after exhausting the endless, yet somehow inconclusive, subsidiary reasons (her flaming red hair, her pleasant disposition, her beautiful nose), finally throws up his hands and replies. "Because that's the way I am! *I* am *I,* that's all."

The religious parallel to the "I am I" situation differs only in that the key word, which a significant tautology always sponsors, is "God" or a reasonable cognate. When "God" is introduced

9. *Religious Language,* p. 43.
10. *Jesus Christ and Mythology* (New York: Scribners, 1958), p. 53.
11. *Religious Language,* p. 51.

into the universe of a particular poem as the commanding "final explanation," the poem becomes literally subjugated to the demands of its own commitment. The poem's structure becomes dependent upon a logic which ought to baffle and confound our common sense so that the desired discernment and subsequent commitment to the claims of the discernment can occur. Perhaps the most illuminating illustration of these remarks is one of George Herbert's most famous and successful poems, "The Collar."

> I struck the board, and cry'd, No more.
>   I will abroad.
>   What? shall I ever sigh and pine?
> My lines and life are free; free as the rode,
>   Loose as the winde, as large as store.
>   Shall I be still in suit?
>   Have I no harvest but a thorn
>   To let me bloud, and not restore
>   What I have lost with cordiall fruit?
>   Sure there was wine
> Before my sighs did drie it: there was corn
>   Before my tears did drown it.
>   Is the yeare onely lost to me?
>   Have I no bayes to crown it?
> No flowers, no garlands gay? all blasted?
>   All wasted?
>   Not so, my heart: but there is fruit,
>   And thou hast hands.
>   Recover all thy sigh-blown age
> On double pleasures: leave thy cold dispute
> Of what is fit, and not. Forsake thy cage,
>   Thy rope of sands,
> Which pettie thoughts have made, and made to thee
>   Good cable, to enforce and draw,
>   And be thy law,
> While thou didst wink and wouldst not see.
>   Away; take heed:
>   I will abroad.
> Call in thy deaths head there: tie up thy fears.
>   He that forbears
>   To suit and serve his need,
>   Deserves his load.
> But as I rav'd and grew more fierce and wilde
>   At every word,

Me thoughts I heard one calling, *Child!*
And I reply'd, *My Lord.*

"The Collar" is expressly a poem about commitment, and the commitment of the final line is evoked by a sudden discernment in the text to the last line which dramatically underscores the abrupt shift in logic which characterizes the experience of faith itself. That the key words *"Child"* and *"My Lord"* possess more than prima facie significance is characteristic of Herbert's technique of weaving doctrine directly into the fabric of his poetry. The ability to understand one's self as a child before God was a quasi-formal test of election in the seventeenth century. Donne, for example, often preached, ". . . that we are able *to cry Abba, Father, by the Spirit of Adoption,* is this testimony, *that we are his children*; if we can truly do that, that testifies for us."[12] It is appropriate in Herbert's poem, therefore, that the conclusion of the intense vocational-spiritual crisis should involve re-assurance of election, but more important to the consideration at hand is the capability of these words to evoke the characteristically religious discernment.

It has often been pointed out that the relatively chaotic metrical scheme of the beginning of "The Collar" intentionally complements the corresponding chaotic condition of the persona's mind. Nevertheless, the poem progresses according to a consistent logic. The question at hand is simply: I am a free agent; why do I continue in a way of life which, for all intents and purposes, is contrary to my very nature? The conduct of the internal debate is highly rational. Commitment is logically revealed as a "rope of sand"; there is even the reasonable counsel that a man usually gets what he deserves, in lines 30-32. There is more than the social pragmatism of a Polonius in these lines. A crisis of the greatest urgency is being endured, and an alternative way of life is being cogently and seriously considered. The full brunt of conventional logic is pressed against an absurd (from the rational point of view) commitment which apparently has no logical justification within the context of the poem, excepting for the moment the final two lines.

What gives meaning to the poem, of course, is the logical

12. *The Sermons of John Donne,* ed. George R. Potter and Evelyn M. Simpson, 10 vols. (Berkeley, 1953-62), V, sermon 2, lines 482-4.

impropriety of the placing of the key words "Child" and "Lord." They do not belong in the language-game of the poem proper. They serve as an affront to the logical structure of the protest. *"Child! "* is no rebuttal at all. It does not answer any of the points raised prior to it, and yet, in another sense, the sense that discernment brings, it answers all those questions and more. "The Collar" exploits as the principle of its construction the collision of two radically disparate logical structures. The consequence of this collision is the disclosure that something more than rationality is at stake. The actual words "Child" and "Lord" lay claim to a commitment radically different from the one with which the persona begins the poem.

"The Collar" is a good example of how object language can be qualified so as to make it proper currency for a religious situation. From any point of view other than the logic of obedience the poem is nonsense. An angry man assesses his vocation and announces to himself that he is fed up. He unleashes a convincing barrage of arguments to support his emotional frustration. Our common-sense expectation is that the arguments will be examined and a decision reached on the basis of their merits. Since no convincing rebuttal is presented, it seems clear that the only course of action is to clear out and take up a new life. But abruptly the common-sense expectation is turned inside out by a bit of apparent irrelevance. Someone is heard calling, *"Child! "* to which our hero mysteriously replies, *"My Lord."* End of poem.

No one, of course, reads "The Collar" with that degree of religious naiveté because the poem encourages, demands even, that the reader be open to two conflicting language patterns. The poem clearly commends "Child" and "Lord" as key words which somehow express much more than their normal denotations. True, the words are traditional members of the Christian vocabulary, and this, of course, would signal their semantic uniqueness, but there is no explicit compulsion that the reader take them in their religious sense *except* that any sense at all is to be made out of the poem. Just as in the case of "The Flower" the reader is forced to accept religious insight under pain of failing to understand the poem on any terms. We might take the situation at the end of "The Collar" in slow motion and try to reconstruct what steps the mind must go through when its expectations have been suddenly confounded by the odd word *"Child! "* Who is calling? *My Lord.* Who is *"My Lord"*? No explicit answer. What kind of Lord could change my mind in the face of such compelling arguments? Ah, yes, this is *The* Lord urging a higher commitment upon me, and so forth. In fact, two language systems have collided in "The Collar." The language of common-sense suddenly meets the language of obedience. Immediately, the problem of setting a priority between them comes up. Simultaneously with this a discernment of what is at stake floods into the reader's consciousness and, hopefully, his lips echo the last words of the poem for himself.

Names, we have seen, play crucial functional roles in scriptural language and in Herbert's poetic devotions because they serve to make the theological vocabulary distinctive. God-talk does not permit a name to remain a mere label because such a thoroughgoing nominalism would drain all possibility of "depth" — depth which, I have been arguing, makes ordinary situations characteristically religious. The religious use of names, therefore, strives at all costs to avoid literalism. In fact, the degree to which religious names point *away* from their objective referends measures the degree of their religious potency.

As an example of the referential potency of religious names, we might take the name of God Himself. A few pages back I had occasion to mention the reverence with which the Jews held the name of God, even to the point of never pronouncing it. We detect this nervousness about the divine name in the third chapter of Exodus. When God identifies Himself to Moses, He employs not so much a name as a description of Himself: "I am that I am." We might have some insight into the divine linguistic strategy here if we consider that "I am that I am" is exactly the kind of analytical tautology that I have cited as expressive of one's ultimate commitment in my discussion of "Affliction (III)." As an evocation of a final explanation, "I am that I am" is a profound disclosure situation. It betrays its logical impropriety by operating less as a name than as a riddle. The reason it does so is not merely the Hebrew injunction against uttering God's name, but because the riddle (the logical impropriety) signals the exhaustion of all conceptual, didactic explanations of the Diety. The riddle appropriately accords with God's mystery. A label would literalize God; it would appropriate Him into the natural world where all proper nouns take clearcut predication and where mystery is anathema.

Other religious names work under the same principle. The words "Child" and "Lord" in "The Collar," for example. Beyond religiously referential proper names there are names that stand for physical objects such as "cross," "altar," "crucifix," and so forth. The cross, to take just one example, is a religious name only when it points far beyond its objective reference to its personal significance for the Christian. "In the Christian faith," writes Carl Michalson, "the constant antecedent of the cross is not a geological formation called Golgotha but Jesus' obedience to the word of God."[13]

There are also names which refer not to things but to experiences which are similarly potent as key religious words: "sin," "grace," "faith," "election," "justification," "salvation," and so forth. All of these names require a contextual understanding in that their meanings are found in their use. They have no magical properties which cause heathens automatically to fall on their knees upon hearing them uttered. What religious names can claim, however, is a fertile collection of connotations which afford them what modish theologians now a days call "hermeneutical potential." As "The Collar" shows us, religious names, when properly placed, have the potential to supersede and tyrannize an existing logical pattern with the new frame of reference they bring with them — the logic of obedience.

The key religious names "Child" and "My Lord" enjoy their appropriate religious interpretation in "The Collar" because the poem ceases to make any sense unless they do. I should also add that some words, while they do not possess the potency of key religious words, are nevertheless highly sensitive to religious activation once their context has been theologically charged. The first part of "The Collar" is saturated with such words which remain theologically dormant until "Child" and "My Lord" wrench them into life. These second-line status religious words include: "Have I no harvest but a *thorn* / To let me *bloud* . . ." "Sure there was *wine*. . ." and so forth. Words like these must be used with great delicacy, for there is always the danger that their latent religiosity

13. *Rationality of Faith*, p. 34.

might give away the surprise of the powerful reversal of logic engineered at the poem's end.

Herbert's particular fascination with the potency and mystery of religious names can be illustrated in "The Odour" also:

How sweetly doth *My Master* sound! *My Master!*
    As Amber-greese leaves a rich sent Unto the taster:
        So do these words a sweet content,
An orientall fragrancie, *My Master.*

With these all day I do perfume my minde,
    My minde ev'n thrust into them both:
        That I might finde
    What cordials make this curious broth,
This broth of smells, that feeds and fats my minde.

My Master, shall I speak? O that to thee
    My servant were a little so,
        As flesh may be;
    That these two words might creep & grow
To some degree of spicinesse to thee!

Then should the Pomander, which was before
    A speaking sweet, mend by reflection,
        And tell me more:
    For pardon of my imperfection
Would warm and work it sweeter then before.

For when *My Master,* which alone is sweet,
    And ev'n in my unworthinesse pleasing,
        Shall call and meet,
    My servant, as thee not displeasing,
That call is but the breathing of the sweet.

This breathing would with gains by sweetning me
    (As sweet things traffick when they meet)
        Return to thee.
    And so this new commerce and sweet
Should all my life employ and busie me.

The meditative matrix of this poem is abundantly apparent not only because its title includes its scriptural source (2 Cor. 2:15), but from the poem's rather obvious indebtedness to François de

Sales' recipe for "iaculatorie prayers" described in *An Introduction to a Devoute Life*. The perfuming of the mind, of which Herbert speaks, the "orientall fragrancie" of the phrase *"My Master,"* the "broth of smells, that feeds and fats my minde," all suggest at least a functional accord with the Salesian practice of ending meditations with a "nosegay of devotion" or "a spiritual posy." St. François recommends that "we should cull out, one or two points which we have found most pleasing to our taste . . . and as it were mentally smell theron all the rest of the day." There is the further counsel to "fasten the inward view of thy soule upon his inestimable sweetnes . . . place him in thy bosome like a sweet-smelling posie." The consequence of this meditation is that "our spirit once giving itself entirelie to the companie, hant, and familiaritie of his God, must needs be all perfumed, with the odiferous ayre of his perfections."[14]

Henry Vaughan's "Unprofitableness" also displays a direct indebtedness to the Salesian trope, when it celebrates the return of God's grace with the joyous realization: "I flourish, and once more / Breath all perfumes, and spice." No doubt taking this cue from Herbert, Vaughan also fixes on the word "spiciness" and permeates his poem with the extended metaphor of smell. It is the irony at the end of Vaughan's poem which sets it apart from "The Odour" because no sweetness results in "Unprofitableness" but rather "a stench, or fog is all / The odour I bequeath."

But there is more than the mere distinction of irony which separates the Herbert and Vaughan poems. Herbert's poem is of a quite different order because the focus of his meditation is not upon an experience of the fresh visit of God to a "sullyed" soul, but upon a name, *"My Master,"* and the corresponding complement it evokes, *"My servant,"* Moreover, the two names are oddly used throughout "The Odour" so as to present themselves as logical improprieties. By objectifying a relationship (master-servant) through the technique of verbal realism, that is, by permitting the physical *words* rather than their denotations to receive the initial logical attention, Herbert manages to sustain a *grammatical* consis-

14. *An Introduction to a Devoute Life,* trans. John Yakesley, 3rd ed. (Rouen, 1614), pp. 132-34, 152-54. Quoted by Martz in *The Poetry of Meditation*, pp. 251-52, 254

tency while throwing *semantic* consistency into chaos. All this, of course, is to the benefit of encouraging a religious situation to occur, precisely because of the strange placing of the key words.

Certain other rhetorical phenomena also become possible through this technique. Not the least are the synaesthetic associations that cleave to the word *"Master"* and the word *"servant,"* which could not have occurred if the focus were upon their denotations. Hence we have: "How sweetly doth *My Master* sound! " with its rich openness to double interpretation, not to mention the logical subtleties of stanzas five and six which make this poem appear particularly "metaphysical."

It hardly seems necessary to defend this poem against charges of insincere artifice, since those elements, which a critic might leap on as "conceited" or even "ingenious" are not the *innovations* of Herbert but rather his *donnés.* The rather remarkable fit of this poem with the meditative practices described by de Sales, combined with the scriptural text, "For we are unto God a sweet savor of Christ . . . ," indicate quite clearly that the originality in this poem is to be found in the ways Herbert manages to place his key words so as to sponsor truly religious situations. In short, the burden of this poem is to provoke insights into the master-servant relationship by "stretching" conventional language to the point where it potentially can yield the "something more" which is the *sine qua non* of any discernment situation.

What are some of the facets of the discernment inherent in "The Odour"? One, which a knowledge of Herbert's technique suggests could not be fortuitous, is the logically improper, but doctrinally pungent, implication of Christ as the Word of God. In the context of the poem, *"Master"* literally is the Word, and it is the Word (Christ) who indeed does "sweetly" sound. Here is a case of a Christian doctrinal truth being structurally rendered instead of didactically told. Resources other than linear verbal logic are exploited by Herbert, contributing even more to the "openness" which is characteristic of religious communication. Another distinctive feature of "The Odour" is its almost chaotic mixing of sense functions. Sound, smell and taste dominate: the sweet sound of *"My Master,"* the "rich sent" of "Amber-greese," the "orientall fragrancie" of *"My Master"* again, the "broth of smells, that feeds and fats" the mind, and the "speaking" and "breathing" sweets. It is a highly sensuous poem, but the really distinctive quality of this sensuousness is its free abandon. The transition from one sense to another is only tenuously logical. Association of ideas seems more in control of the rapid shifts from sweet sound to "rich sent" to "broth of smells" to "spiciness." True, this sort of eclectic sensuousness might be explained simply by the conventional definitions of the metaphysical conceit, that it is the nature of the conceit to bind together incongruous elements and experiences. But this really does not do justice to what Herbert attempts to achieve in this poem. "The Odour" is not a case where, as Joan Bennett describes metaphysical poetry, "emotions are shaped and expressed by logical reasoning, and both sound and picture are subservient to this end."[15] Quite to the contrary, "The Odour" performs under its vocational charge to create situations of religious discernment which simultaneously invite commitment. The conduct of its language is dictated not by descriptively arrived at "rules" of metaphysical behavior, but by the requirements of Christian disclosure. Since Christian disclosure is more or less effectively blocked by empirically- and causally-oriented language, Christianity is compelled to adapt that ordinary language to meet its unique ends.

Rather than comparing the kaleidoscopic sensuousness of "The Odour" to the characteristics of the metaphysical poem, it is more rewarding to examine its similarity to traditional Biblical language. It would not be difficult to point to almost any passage in the Song of Solomon for a comparison, the description of the lover, for example:

> His eyes are as the eyes of the doves by the rivers of waters, washed with milk and fitly set:
> His cheeks are as a bed of spices, as sweet flowers: his lips like lilies, dropping sweet smelling myrrh.

Some might object that the Song of Solomon is hardly a fair comparison because it is not strictly a religious piece of literature but a secular love poem adapted to a religious purpose. In that case, the more specifically Christian language of the New Testament might be more convincing, particularly if we avoid even those passages which are overtly poetic in order to press our point that the struc-

---

15. *Four Metaphysical Poets,* 2nd ed. (New York: Vintage, 1960), p. 12.

ture of God-talk strives in both poetry and prose to evoke discernments through logical impropriety. An example cited by Ramsey is Acts 5:30, 31:

> Jesus whom ye slew, hanging him on a tree . . . him did God exalt with his right hand to be a Prince *and* a *Saviour* for to give repentance to Israel, and remission of sins.

Ramsey sees in passages like this one "a riotous mixture of phrases" which belong "intrinsically to . . . many different logical areas." He sees this "riotous mixing" as "in effect a rough and ready attempt to secure that special logical impropriety needed to express the Christian message."[16] The words "Prince," "Saviour," "tree" have, of course, become metaphorical petrifacts to those reared in the Judeo-Christian culture, but from a coldly logical examination they do exhibit the sort of oddity that Ramsey claims is prerequisite for a characteristically religious situation. The oddity of the synaesthetic revelry in "The Odour" seems to fit into the same pattern. Herbert was not interested primarily in the logical behavior of his words; he was interested in evoking the same sort of disclosure he achieved in "The Collar" — a personal, intimate, perhaps even existential realization of what it is to be a child-servant of a lord-master.

The structure of the language discernible in Herbert's poetic devotions, then, is designed, it would seem, not to inform and not primarily to please. Rather, it displays a constant fidelity to its vocation which is to create verbal situations capable of evoking the experience of the presence of God. In its vocational context, God-talk is not structured to serve the requirements of beauty or logic, but to prepare the way for Apocalypse. It only pretends to walk the horizontal plane of cause-and-effect logic; its real mission is to draw attention to the vertical heights and depths normally ignored by conventional language because they are pictorially inexpressible.

16. *Religious Language,* p. 178.

Chapter Five: "The Sacrifice"

When William Empson selected George Herbert's "The Sacrifice" as an example of his seventh type of ambiguity, he described the poem as "unique as achieved by successive fireworks of contradiction, and a mind jumping like a flea."[1] Although his main purpose was to demonstrate that the poem "assumes, as does its theology, the existence of conflicts, but its business is to state a generalized solution of them,"[2] he left the very strong impression that the "fireworks" and the "jumping fleas" should be credited to "Herbert's method." With some justification, Rosemund Tuve saw occasion to take Empson's "New Critical" approach to task by pointing out his error in ascribing to Herbert many of the effects which belonged to older liturgical and literary traditions.[3] According to Miss Tuve, "The Sacrifice" owes its dramatic structure to the traditional *Improperia*, the Reproaches of Christ spoken from the Cross, part of the liturgies of the Good Friday service and Holy Week, and the Pleading of Christ tradition. Consequently, she presses the case that the alleged Metaphysical roughness in Herbert's poem is actually the result of "borrowed" devices, particularly the traditional paradoxes of the liturgy and "sundry medieval lyrics."[4]

1. William Empson, *Seven Types of Ambiguity*, 2nd ed. (London, 1947), p. 226. Quotations from "The Sacrifice" are from F. E. Hutchinson's edition of the *Works* (Oxford, 1941), pp. 26-34; my references are to line numbers.
2. Empson, p. 227.
3. Louis Martz has risen to the defense of Empson by remarking that Miss Tuve "has gone . . . too far in arguing that Herbert's 'Sacrifice' displays 'precisely the tone of the "Reproaches" and of sundry medieval lyrics' " (*The Poetry of Meditation*, 2nd. ed. [New Haven: Yale University Press, 1962], p. 91), and Malcolm MacKenzie Ross, in a display of the *via media* worthy of a Hooker, has declared: "It is a mistake in critical method to read the Christian paradoxes of Herbert as though he had invented them or as though he had merely inherited them" (*Poetry and Dogma* [New Brunswick, N.J.: Rutgers University Press, 1954], pp. 6-7).
4. See Miss Tuve's *A Reading of George Herbert* (London, 1952), pp.

Whatever degree of originality we wish to assign to Herbert's part in "The Sacrifice," it is difficult to quarrel with Miss Tuve's general conclusion that "the notion of a monologue spoken by Christ, the notion of what such a monologue should contain, the symbolically used Old Testament refrain, the special mingling of contradictory emotions in the speaker, and the general poetic tone of the whole, were traditional for many years before Herbert used them."[5] The very fact that "The Sacrifice" is so deeply embedded in liturgical tradition, that it does "assume, as does its theology, the existence of conflicts," added to the critical agreement that the poem boasts, if not "fireworks" and "jumping fleas," at least kinetic ambiguities and paradoxes, makes very plausible the possibility that it is not the literary style of a particular poem under consideration but the very structure of God-talk itself.

"The Sacrifice" is a poetic devotion which is also a reasonably pure specimen of religious language. The fact it is highly derivative and relatively free of the eccentricities of its particular author[6] makes it a good model for a structural analysis of the language of devotional poetry. It must be borne in mind that such an analysis assumes more than a mere aesthetic interest in devotional poetry: it recognizes that such poetry, like prayer, has a vocation — to evoke a characteristically religious awareness of the presence of God.[7] If it is not always read in that spirit today, it is

19-99, and "On Herbert's 'Sacrifice,' " *Kenyon Review,* 12 (1950), 51-75. Rosemary Freeman shares Miss Tuve's opinion on the origin of the dramatic method of "The Sacrifice"; see *English Emblem Books* (London, 1948), pp. 160-62.

5. Tuve, *A Reading of George Herbert,* p. 47.

6. Miss Tuve notes that "Herbert's poem "The Sacrifice" is full of minute shocks, of unexpected connexions, sudden recoils in the emotion described or produced — and it is this temper or tone . . . *which he inherited* [italics mine]" (*A Reading of George Herbert,* p. 41).

7. Geddes MacGregor (*Aesthetic Experience in Religion* [London: MacMillan, 1947], p. 212) remarks: "The *raison d'être* of a 'work of art' is to stimulate the aesthetic experience that has been . . . deposited in it. The *raison d'être* of a 'holy thing' is to stimulate experience in a certain *direction,* namely (in the long run) mystical union with God." Helen C. White's *Prayer and Poetry* (Latrobe, Pa., 1960) is also illuminating on the relationship of worship and poetry.

most probable that George Herbert intended his "Sacrifice" to be received with more than an aesthetic satisfaction.

The first stanza of the poem serves as a structural model for those that follow:

> *Oh alle ye, who passe by,* whose eyes and minde
> To worldly things are sharp, but to me blinde;
> To me, who took eyes that I might you finde:
> Was ever grief like mine?

There are no grammatical or syntactical problems with the language of this stanza, but its meaning might perhaps give us pause. Even here, however, the familiarity of Christian claims can easily blunt our appreciation of the peculiar demands that the assertion places on us. Suspending for a moment our presuppositions concerning the status and power of the as yet unnamed persona, we might justifiably inquire why passersby should be expected to make a more discrimination between "worldly things" and him. At best it seems a piece of enigmatic casuistry; the first two lines scold, but the reason for the scolding is cloudy, There seems to be a pettish accusation of misdirected loyalty made against the passersby who allegedly pay more heed to worldly things than to human suffering. But despite the insinuation by the persona that due respect has been withheld from him, the first two lines of the stanza can be interpreted within the limits of a purely moral situation: a suffering man ignored by callous, materialistic self-seekers. It is line three that suddenly infects the stanza with an odd taint. The status of the persona is mysteriously qualified. Our initial understanding of the situation is confounded by the powers assigned to him, which clearly transcend mortal categories. What kind of being "takes eyes" in order to search out men? Why should the persona be seeking men out? Some special insight or knowledge is required to comprehend the new status of the situation. We are no longer dealing with a purely moral circumstance; suddenly a theological claim has been injected, and we find ourselves confronting a collision of two language patterns. Once the persona is implicitly identified as divine, the previous logic of morality runs at loggerheads with a rival theological one.

Significantly, however, no "theological" words are employed. There is little or no figurative play with the language. Indeed, the sense of the stanza, from the standpoint of its religious meaning, depends upon a *literal* understanding of the words. It is from the semantic confusion of the colliding language patterns that ambiguities and paradoxes spring, rendering the resultant language structure its religious cast.

These ambiguities and paradoxes, however, are not quite those of which Empson speaks. Empson understands the task of "The Sacrifice" to "state a generalized solution" of the conflicts inherent in Christian theology, but the aim of religious language is precisely the opposite of this. Rather than considering the conflicts as flaws to be cleared up, it deliberately cultivates them for the purpose of obstructing normal patterns of thought. Religious language seeks no solution, for any *inferred* reconciliation of condictions would be the very opposite of what truly religious communications seeks — an awareness of God, revealed through noninferential discernment. John Donne, we remember from Chapter Two, was aware of the distinction between these two forms of apprehension when he preached: ". . . a regenerate Christian, being now a *new Creature,* hath also *a new facultie of Reason*: and so believeth the Mysteries of Religion, but of another Reason, than as a meere natural Man, he believed naturall and morall things."[8] In order to express a religious situation so that it can be properly comprehend by the "new facultie of Reason," language must be put to special use. It must be so used as to exploit logical scandals which occur when moral and theological situations collide.

At this point it would be helpful to speak more specifically of the peculiar properties of statements about God so that we can better gauge their distinctiveness from mere moral assertions. I. M. Crombie has isolated what he calls "the anomalies of the formal properties of theological statements."[9] There are two such anomalies and both are clearly illustrated in the stanza we are considering. The first is that theological statements insist that their subject (God or his divine surrogate) be interpreted *as if* He were a particular individual even though the conduct of such statements

8. *The Sermons of John Donne,* ed. George R. Potter and Evelyn M. Simpson, 10 vols. (Berkeley, 1953-62), III, sermon 17, lines 407-13.

9. "The Possibility of Theological Statements," *Religious Language and the Problem of Religious Knowledge,* ed. Ronald E. Santoni (Bloomington, Ind.: Indiana University Press, 1968), p. 90.

differs obviously from that of all other statements. In this stanza, for example, Christ is spoken of as a particular man who suffers grief for a presumed affront of some sort. However, the phrase "who took eyes what I might you finde" baffles our comprehension of this particular man from any literal point of view. He becomes a mysterious entity with superhuman powers who claims an obligation of an intensity greater than that which we might owe a friend, relative, or other mortal.

Crombie's second anomaly is that in theological statements everyday words are not used according to their everyday senses. In other words, such an assertion as "God loves us" is only a crude approximation of the claim most Christians make concerning God's dealings with men. As was pointed out before, even more havoc is made of everyday denotations when Christians talk about Creation *ex nihilo* or "God in Three Persons." The third line of our stanza is cut of the same cloth: "To me, who took eyes that I might you finde." Although we might dismiss this phrase as mere metonymy, such a glib rhetorical explanation fails to do justice to the depth of Christian dogma which Herbert obviousiy intended to express in the line. There is much more religious significance in the assertion than literal analysis can yield. In short, the two anomalies which attend the use of theological statements teach us that religious language presumes to speak of and to a Being which exists outside the world of time and space to which the patterns of everyday discourse are geared. The "reality" which "The Sacrifice" hopes to reveal is a reality normally inaccessible to causal patterns of thought. What the poem requires and what the poem indeed does exploit is a language, to use Erich Auerbach's term again, that is "fraught with background."[10] The poem does not aim at making inferences but attempts to evoke discernments. It is not new information that Herbert's poem seeks to initiate poetically, but a sense of "depth." That such a sense of depth is penultimate to revelation and commitment testifies to the significance of the *vocational* role of the devotional poem.

Virtually all of the stanzas of "The Sacrifice" follow the same pattern as the first: one or two lines dealing with a situation

10. *Mimesis: The Representation of Reality in Western Literature*, trans. Willard Trask (Princeton: Princeton University Press, 1953), p. 9.

of moral injustice are penetrated by an anomalous line or lines which upsets or reverses the anticipated dénouement. In other words, the intruding line establishes a new context; a different pattern (more powerful than the first because of its theological credentials) is permitted to overpower and tyrannize the meaning and structure of the stanza as a whole. A second example, taken at random, bears out the validity of the formula:

> Heark how they crie aloud still, *Crucifie:*
> *It is not fit he live a day,* they crie,
> Who cannot live lesse than eternally:
> Was ever grief like mine?

It is unimportant that the central section of this stanza is derivative. What is significant is that again the first two lines are theologically neutral. They could have been screamed in moral outrage at any thief by any man. It is very human language and its logic is decidedly ethical. The third line, however, takes hold of us with its "oddness." Although it is a simple relative clause, from the outset it excites curious options through the ambiguity of its reference. *Who* is it who lives eternally? Syntactical logic leads us to *"he,"* but suddenly we confront a knot of paradoxes: an eternal one who is not fit to live a day, the crucifixion of one who lives eternally, and the implication of the rational contrariness of the stanza as a whole. Once again the anomalies of the formal properties of theological statements are exploited in order to propel a basically moral situation into a theological context. Paradox is called upon to do more than mere rhetoric or poetry might require; it is assigned a vocational role.

If we can accept for the moment the hypothesis that the real distinctiveness of "The Sacrifice" derives from the collision or interpenetration of rival language systems, we can then go on to inquire about the nature of such paradoxical communication as it functions within a religious context. A model, we remember, serves to anchor an account of religious experience upon empirical fact. This means that a proper model in religious discourse will always be an experience, situation, or object that is rooted in phenomenal reality. In "The Sacrifice," for example, we could identify as models those lines in each individual stanza which conform to mundane (usually moral) experiences: lines which restrict themselves to ethical situations, phenomenal objects, or human experiences as opposed to theological claims beyond the limits of space and time. The best models are those which parallel religious faith on a worldly- level by inviting one's commitment: a lover's loyalty to his beloved, a patriot's devotion to his country, or a moralist's concern for duty. The refrain of "The Sacrifice" ("Was ever grief like mine? ") might be considered a case of a sustained model which is ultimately "qualified" in the final stanza.

The function of a "qualifier," we remember, is to deepen the significance of a mundane commitment in such a way that its religious parallel (which cannot be expressed other than obliquely) falls on one's consciousness as a disclosure. It confounds one's customary rational stance toward the situation and forces the pursuit of alternative routes to understanding. Relating this once again to "The Sacrifice," we could call that line (or lines) in each individual stanza which imposes the theological claim upon the other model lines the qualifier. It must be stressed, however, that a qualifier never *describes* a model as an adjective does; it *does not* provide additional information about the model. Rather, it has a dynamic effect. It provokes a "logical impropriety" by deliberately baffling the normal rules of cause-effect logic. In short, the qualifier is the anomalous line.

While models and qualifiers can be seen operating in all the stanzas of "The Sacrifice," the following appears to contain an additional irony not shared by all, making it perhaps a more conspicuous specimen:

> Behold, they spit on me in scornful wise,
> Who by my spittle gave the blind man eies,
> Leaves his blindness to my enemies:
>   Was ever grief like mine?

The first line, of course, is the model. It urges no theological claim and is a straightforward statement of fact. The following two lines are qualifiers because they introduce the anomaly. The narrator is set off as strangely remarkable by a series of crescendoing contrasts. The spittle he receives, which is inefficacious, unsalutary, and vulgar, is presented as a foil for the spittle which the narrator is capable of producing. It becomes the medium through which the divinity of the narrator is suggested and through which a fundamental Christian claim is expressed. It requires special spittle indeed to cure blindness, far more special than medical knowledge of the time was cognizant. Hence, the model of the stanza provides an empirical base (spittle) which is subsequently qualified when related to the narrator (medicinal spittle) so as to create just such a logical impropriety of which Ramsey speaks.

The contrast of blindnesses intensifies the oddness of this stanza. The literal use of the word "blind" in the second line serves as a model for the theological charged "blindness" of line three. Blindness to the things of this world is played against the blindness to God, and the confrontation of the two disparate referents creates a logical scandal which precipitates, according to Ramsey's system, a series of "stories."[11] As the mind attempts to reconcile apparent irreconcilables, it is invited to follow a chain of meditations which is directionally controlled by the qualifier. One of Ramsey's own examples is helpful. A traditional characterization of God has been the term "Infinite Wisdom." Identifying "Wisdom" as the model of this phrase, we notice that the qualifier, "Infinite," creates the desired "logical impropriety" and eventually causes a qualitative transformation of the whole phrase to occur. As we initially confront the phrase, we see that "Wisdom" is plain enough but that the addition of "Infinite" baffles any literal appreciation of the phrase. "Wisdom," as a model, suggests a certain direction for our mind to follow, but when it is qualified by "Infinite," we are forced to acknowledge that the word is only a model standing in for the real experience which we seek. We must go on and on in the prescribed direction, thinking about wisdom and infinitude, until finally the "light dawns" and the situation takes on the sought-after "depth."[12] Ramsey calls this occurrence a "disclosure" and insists that even though it appears close to a psychological explanation of how religious language communicates, it is not "purely subjective" since every experience is an experience of something.[13] The similarity of this procedure with traditional techniques of spiritual meditation does much to support its vocational relevance and to suggest that there is much more than mere poetic technique involved.

The two blindnesses operate according to the same general

11. *Religious Language* (New York: Macmillan, 1963), pp. 63-7, 91.
12. Ramsey, p. 30.
13. Ramsey, p. 26.

pattern as "infinite Wisdom." The worldly blindness of line two (the model) is qualified by a strangely "figurative" blindness in line three. Through contemplation of literal blindness we are led through a series of stories of what blindness really means. Figurative blindness (Christ's bestowal of blindness upon his enemies) causes us to understand that blindness is just a model, and our further contemplation hopefully results in a disclosure when the "ice will break, the light dawn, and a characteristically religious situation . . . . [is] evoked."[14] In this case the disclosure involves several revelations which can be approximately translated: (1) a realization of the divinity of the narrator, (2) an acknowledgment that the enemies of the narrator are blind to reality, and (3) that Reality is not the things of this world but the narrator himself, Jesus Christ.[15]

In several stanzas of "The Sacrifice" the structure has been deliberately designed to sustain complexity not only through "logical improprieties" but through grammatical ones as well. In such cases it can be said that religious language exploits syntactical complexity not to create, but *to avoid* misunderstandings. An example touched on by both Empson and Miss Tuve serves well:

> Some said, that I the Temple to the floore
> In three days raz'd, and raised as before.
> Why, he that built the world can do much more:
> Was ever grief like mine?

A grammatical impropriety serves in this instance to evoke the characteristically Christian discernment latent in the stanza. There is not much sense to line three unless identification is made be-

14. Ramsey, p. 74.

15. The mode of extra-logical communication suggested here is very similar to what Phillip Wheelwright has called "tensive language." One kind of tension in language, he says, "arises from the overtones of universality that may be implied in an utterance. Such tension is typically found in the relationship, perhaps uncertain and wavering, between the situation as described or the succession of images as presented, and the stray glimpses of truth they suggest without actually stating" (*Metaphor and Reality* [Bloomington, Ind.: Indiana University Press, 1962], p. 55). Religious language as Ramsey sees it varies from Wheelwright's definition of "tensive language" only to the degree that specific religious dogma effectively tyrannizes the behavior of the language which works to reveal its truth.

tween the pronouns "he" and "I." Confusion exists in all contexts except that of Christian dogma. The recalcitrance of all solutions save the one which is distinguished by grammatical inconsistency leads to the Christian disclosure of *communicatio idiomatum* (hypostasis).

Another example of the same principle occurs in the stanza beginning with line 129. Here, once again, pronouns operate to create a complexity which functions to avoid secular misunderstanding. Although the poem has been consistently in the first person up to this point, it shifts in this one isolated instance to the third:

> They buffet him, and box him as they list,
> Who grasps the earth and heaven with his fist,
> And never yet, whom he would punish, miss'd:
> Was ever grief like mine?

Once again, grammatical confusion points the way toward a disclosure of the dogma of the Hypostatic Union. The "I" of the poem suddenly and mysteriously transforms into "him," moreover a "him" who possesses the superhuman power of grasping "earth and heaven with his fist." A language pattern of moral logic in line one is upended in line two by a key theological claim, but even this integration of the two logical patterns is intensified by the grammatical "oddness" of the entire stanza when measured against the whole context.

If there is merit in regarding "The Sacrifice" from a doctrinal rather than a mere moral point of view, then there is special significance to Ian Ramsey's contention that "the greatest mistake anyone can make is to think that hypostatic union describes some fact in the way that ordinary public languages do."[16] To see "The Sacrifice" as a resolution of conflicts through the instrumentality of poetry is to make the mistake of which Ramsey speaks. Quite to the contrary, "The Sacrifice" is successful because it leaves the conflicts intact; the *sine qua non* of religious disclosure is a sustained complexity.

The sustained complexity of Herbert's poem is supported by the doctrine of the Incarnation in that Jesus Christ becomes the object of two competing language structures. On the one hand,

16. Ramsey, p. 193.

Herbert describes Christ in quite empirical terms: He undergoes grief, He feels injustice, He bleeds, He weeps, and He experiences physical pain. On the other hand, language is ascribed to Christ which has no empirical basis at all: He commands even those who kill Him, He lives eternally, He grasps heaven and earth with His fist. One language is appropriate currency for man, the other for God, and yet both claim legitimacy in the poem. Clearly, the structure of "The Sacrifice" reveals a linguistic hypostasis which succeeds, in its way, as a "model" for the Divine Hypostasis. No other way is practical for evoking a proper religious appreciation of the hypostatic union, for divine mystery cannot be expected to be described objectively. God-ness plus Man-ness do not sum Jesus Christ. That would be a literal or pictorial conclusion. The very opposite of literalness is required to evoke the truly religious discernment that is required.

Miss Tuve has properly chided Empson for his overly literal interpretation of the stanza which begins with line 20:[17]

> O all ye who passe by, behold and see;
> Man stole the fruit, but I must climbe the tree;
> The tree of life to all, but onely me:
> Was ever grief like mine?

The theological qualifier in this stanza is the exclusionary phrase: "but onely me." Once Christ is afforded a distinction from the rest of mankind, a discernment into the significance of the Atonement begins. More important, however, is how easily Empson is seduced into a disastrous literalism by the "pictorial clarity" (Miss Tuve's words) of the stanza. He remarks, "Jesus seems a child in this metaphor, because he is the Son of God, because he can take the apples without actually stealing (though there is some doubt about this), because of the practical and domestic associations of such a necessity, and because he is evidently smaller than Man, or at any rate Eve, who could pluck the fruit without climbing."[18] Miss Tuve is certainly right when she objects that "symbolic writing (including Herbert's) is confusing only when we read symbol as picture, when we allow the concrete particulars of garden and tree to carry us, by connotation, into alien contexts dependent on

17. *A Reading of George Herbert*, pp. 81 ff.
18. Empson, p. 232.

our individual fancies."[19] She fails, however, to appreciate the positive value of the ambiguity of the stanza. It is one thing to explain away all difficulties by pointing out the obvious familiarity that a seventeenth-century audience would have with cross-tree identifications and climb-ascent connotations, but is another to recognize ambiguity in terms of its potential to initiate meditative inquiries leading to disclosures of a nonpictorial sort. Nor can Empson be credited with appreciating the distinctively religious structure of the language of "The Sacrifice" when he places that poem into the category of his seventh ambiguity by suggesting it as an instance of poetry being used to resolve conflict.[20] Neither is "The Sacrifice" a resolution of a conflict, nor is any individual stanza a resolution of a conflict. To understand the poem in this way is to be captive to a pictorial response to conflicting images. To understand the poem with its vocational (as well as aesthetic) charge in mind is to appreciate the total experience it offers.

Miss Tuve contends that "nothing we can do to this poem can prevent it from being a poem about man seen as guilty of wrongdoing, and faced with the choice of redemption."[21] This conclusion undoubtedly emerges from her appreciation of the continual ironic contrasts between God's omnipotence and man's weakness which saturate the poem. Such a conclusion, however, reveals a predominantly anthropological rather than theological assessment of the poem's intention upon us. It would seem from the structure of the stanzas, where the meeting of two language patterns occurs, that the real subject of this poem is a crucial piece of Christian dogma — the Hypostatic Union.

The argument that I have been pursuing, that devotional literature such as "The Sacrifice" reveals a language structure which is perforce unique because of the anomalies which its subject generates, does not imply that the authors of such literature worked explicitly toward such a formal pattern in writing their poems. To the contrary, the fact that they were striving to exploit beauty to assist them in reaching a higher vocational goal — the

19. *A Reading of George Herbert*, p. 88.
20. Empson, p. 193.
21. *A Reading of George Herbert*, p. 96.

awareness of God — literally forced them into the sort of odd formal structures which would bring about characteristically religious situations. It can be justifiably said that Herbert's instinctive sensitivity to the unusual requirements of Christian expression accounts for the inventiveness he does show in the poem. His presence, however, hardly disturbs the religious structuring of the borrowings he so nimbly assembled and arranged in order to produce "The Sacrifice."

Chapter Six: Milton's God

A poetic devotion is very much like a prayer. It is a direct attempt to communicate with God. Hence, it is easy to understand why the demands of religious utility must supersede and determine the aesthetic and moral activity of such a poem. The issue is not so clear-cut with less direct Christian expressions such as *Paradise Lost.* What is the overriding intention of this epic or other Christian epics like it? Is it merely an ethical narrative in religious dress, a metaphysical blueprint exploiting Christian paraphernalia, a classical epic in the style of Virgil or Homer which just "happens" to have settled on a Christian subject, or is it an instance of genuine God-talk calculated to precipitate characteristically religious situations which at least potentially hold a sense of the presence of God? Such is the concern of the next three chapters.

Rudolf Bultmann's program of demythologizing the Christian faith is a twentieth-century attempt to rescue religious language from the blight of a demeaning literalism. Bultmann identifies language which has degenerated into literalism as "myth" and defines "mythology" as "any manner of representation in which the unworldly and divine appears as the worldly and human — or, in short, in which the transcendent appears as the immanent."[1] Myth is rampant, unchecked anthropomorphism, as Bultmann sees it; it mistakes metaphor for reality. The most dangerous consequence of myth is that it frustrates the normal operation of religious language by encouraging an obtuse insensitivity to the way God-talk works. In a word, myth robs religious expression of "hermeneutical potential."

Technically, hermeneutics is the science of interpretation and explanation, but, according to Heidegger's bizarre etymology, it takes its name from the Olympian God Hermes, who was the herald and messenger of the Gods.[2] It is not difficult to see why

---

1. *Kerygma and Myth,* ed. H. W. Bartsch, trans. R. H. Fuller (New York: Harper Torchbook, 1961), p. 10, n. 2.
2. *Unterwegs zur Sprache,* 2nd ed. (Pfullingen, 1960), pp. 121 f. Carl

many modern theologians use the term to describe the special way
the Word of God behaves in the course of transmitting itself to
humans. In effect, the science of hermeneutics is the science of
God-talk. In its role of guardian of religious mystery, it is the natural enemy of all mythological thinking which, in Schubert Ogden's
words, " 'objectifies' and thus speaks in 'objective' statements
about a reality that is not an 'object.' " Ogden goes on to say that
when myth speaks about the transcendent power of God, it "reduces it to just one more factor in the known and disposable
world. It 'objectifies' the transcendent and thereby transforms
what is really a qualitative difference from the world into a mere
difference of degree."[3] Recalling Auerbach's distinction between
epic and biblical styles, we can perhaps dramatize for ourselves the
process of myth-making by imagining how the Bible would read if
it were re-written in Homeric epic style. Divine mystery would be
translated into worldly clarity.

In the event some might be inclined to dismiss the threat of
religious mythologizing as a peculiarly modern phenomenon, I ask
them to compare Bultmann's position with those lines in which
John Donne once lamented the objectifying advances of the New
Philosophy in the seventeenth century:

> Man hath weav'd out a net, and this net throwne
> Upon the heavens, and now they are his owne.
> Loth to go up the hill, or labor thus
> To go to heaven, we make heaven come to us.[4]

What is it to mythologize if it is not to bring the divine to human
terms — to "make heaven come to us"?

Many might reasonably argue that Donne's lines are an apt
description of Milton's achievement in *Paradise Lost,* that that epic
is, in Bultmann's sense of the word, pure myth, that it lacks hermeneutical potential. It is not difficult to conceive the woven
"net" as the epic's grandiloquent "answerable style" or the cap-
tured "heavens" as a conceptual reduction of divine mystery to

---

Michalson also points out that "after preaching at Lystra, Paul was called
Hermes by the citizens 'because he was the chief speaker' (Acts 14:12)" (*The
Rationality of Faith* [New York: Scribners, 1963], p. 87, n. 30).

    3. *Christ Without Myth* (New York: Harper and Row, 1961), pp. 25-26.

    4. *The First Anniversarie,* "An Anatomy of the World," lines 279-83.

common-sense, all for the purpose of helping men sort out their *ethical* confusions. While we can easily understand the mission of the poetic devotion as a meditative exercise of the human will directed toward the Beatific Vision, a willful, howbeit poetic, laboring "up the hill," Milton's epic, one might argue, is a linguistic kidnapping of the Divine, a flooding out of God's mystery in the very literal light of the natural reason. Something very akin to this view lingers in J. B. Broadbent's complaint that Milton's "normal approach to God was an attempt — like Victorian doubters — to get him down to his own level for debate."[5] Lord David Cecil makes the charge even more explicit: "Milton was not essentially a religious poet. He was a philosopher rather than a devotee. His imagination was lucid and concrete, unlit by heavenly gleams; theology was to him a superior branch of political science, the rule of reason and the moral law as exhibited in the cosmos."[6] The issue might profitably be posed as to whether *Paradise Lost* is a metaphysical system or a religious poem.

My concern, obviously enough, will be to see how an examination of the conduct of Milton's language in the epic might resolve this issue. If *Paradise Lost* can claim any hermeneutical potential, its language would be the place to look for it. Is there any evidence of God-talk in the poem? Are there any instances which can be legitimately described as discernment-commitment situations? Is *Paradise Lost* a truly religious poem or merely a poem about a religious subject?

A number of fairly recent critics have labored hard, with varying success, to assess the quality of the religious dimension (if any) that resides in the epic. Isabel MacCaffrey, for one, sees *Paradise Lost* as "virtual myth" (a literary use of the term not to be confused with Bultmann's religious employment of it), contending that "the poet whose subject is myth strives to promote . . . not learning but knowledge; to evoke no surprise but acknowledgment; to produce not development but revela-

5. "Milton's Heaven," *Milton's Epic Poetry*, ed. C. A. Patrides (Harmondsward, Middlesex: Penguin, 1967), p. 136.

6. *The Oxford Book of Christian Verse* (Oxford: Oxford University Press, 1940), p. xxi.

tion . . ."[7] In effect, Mrs. MacCaffrey's strategy is to turn an apparent liability (*Paradise Lost*'s alleged lack of metaphorical expression) into a stunning hermeneutical asset: "The myth, far from being a symbolic version of some distant truth, is itself the model of which everyday reality is in some sense the symbol."[8]

Anne Davidson Ferry also examines Milton's style for religious depth and claims that the narrative voice of *Paradise Lost* speaks in inspired language that can "envision for us what is beyond our vision."[9] She goes on to explain that the style itself is a miracle like the heavenly inspiration breathed into the poet. It is 'unpremeditated' not because it is unconscious, but because it is mysterious, more than human, a gift of grace. We are meant to be aware of it, to feel its intensity, its uniqueness, its mystery, because these qualities express the poem's meaning."[10] While Mrs. Ferry and Mrs. MacCaffrey speak of Milton's style as promoting mystery and revelation, consequences which my own position can only applaud, both their cases seem to rest rather heavily upon the debatable notion of Milton as a prophet and seer, Mrs. MacCaffrey doing William Blake the honor of claiming his "vision matched Milton's in apocalyptic power."[11]

Stanley Fish's position places less importance on Milton as "seer," but assigns an equally remarkable ingenuity to Milton's stylistic tactics. Less impressed by the miraculous mystery of the epic's language than by its calculated employment, Fish argues that "Milton's purpose is to educate the reader to an awareness of his position and responsibilities as a fallen man, and to a sense of the distance which separates him from the innocence once his." Employing something close to existential strategy, Milton, according to Fish, tries "to re-create in the mind of the reader . . . the drama of the Fall, to make him fall again exactly as Adam did with Adam's troubled clarity, that is to say, 'not deceived.' "[12] If

7. *Paradise Lost as "Myth"* (Cambridge, Mass.: Harvard University Press, 1959), pp. 44-45.

8. *Ibid.*, p. 39.

9. Anne Davidson Ferry, *Milton's Epic Voice: The Narrator in Paradise Lost* (Cambridge, Mass.: Harvard University Press, 1963), p. 6.

10. *Ibid.*, p. 18.

11. MacCaffrey, p. 31.

12. Stanley Fish, *Surprised By Sin: The Reader in Paradise Lost* (London and New York: St. Martin's, 1967), p. 1.

Fish has a major contribution to make to the discussion of hermeneutics in *Paradise Lost,* it is his notion that Milton deliberately deceives us with metaphor and rhetoric only to attach authorial "disclaimers" which point out to us that it was precisely our fallen sinfulness which made the metaphor and rhetoric so attractive to us in the first place.

All three critics, MacCaffrey, Ferry and Fish show concern for the religious vocational role *Paradise Lost* has to play in that they all speak either of the epic's ability to evoke revelation or to awaken conscience. On the other hand, their positions all seem committed to an assumption about the epic's language which tends to conflict with the principles of God-talk: that the language of *Paradise Lost* operates as a kind of moral barometer, that is, that the spiritual status of each of the characters in the poem is revealed by the language he uses. This assumption compromises God-talk's autonomy by perceiving it as merely a device supervised by the *internal* decorum of the poem. God-talk thereby is subsumed under Milton's literary genius rather than understood as an independent phenomenon of the religious experience.

Language as an ethical indicator is an apparently plausible notion and finds plenty of support from the commonly held convictions of Puritan pulpit rhetoric.[13] Plain language, because it is innocent of the artificial adornment of rhetoric and metaphor, is more spiritually pure and religiously appropriate than ornate language which, of course, offers more opportunity for deception and is therefore of the devil. This assumption conveniently justifies the unpleasantness of Milton's God (particularly in His monologue in Book Three) on the grounds that He speaks the way a Puritan sensibility would expect Him to speak: with hard, plain, non-metaphorical, authoritative language. If we should object that such austere stylistics hardly invite religious discernment, not to mention commitment, we receive the admonishment that we are not seventeenth-century Puritans and, therefore, cannot judge the effect of God's "epic" talk upon the Puritan mind.

It is symmetrically pleasing and morally reassuring to know

13. See, for example: W. Fraser Mitchell, *English Pulpit Oratory from Andrewes to Tillotson* (London, 1932), or M. M. Knappen, *Tudor Puritanism* (Chicago, 1933). William Haller has much to say on the point throughout *The Rise of Puritanism* (New York: Harper Torchbook, 1957), esp. pp. 130-32.

that we can trust style to keep our ethical values in order as we read *Paradise Lost*: Satan speaks a language with rhetoric and metaphor; God, the unfallen angels, and prelapsarian man speak a pure tongue. Style, according to this view, polices the internal consistency of the epic and elicits from us an admiration of Milton's literary genius in accomplishing the trick so neatly and effectively. No doubt our admiration of Homer springs from similar decorous conspiracies of style and ethics. But we might ask ourselves, in the midst of our admiration, is this really a *religious* style that we are admiring or perhaps rather an unparalleled feat of aesthetic decorum? We ought to ask this question because the whole notion of language functioning as spiritual litmus has the ironic consequence of pitting style *against* Christian dogma, suggesting (against evidence from Scripture) that the tools of rhetoric and poetry are inherently sinful. From the reader's point of view, that language in *Paradise Lost* which has been calculated to inspire and affect him the most turns out not to be the Word of God at all but the language of sin. In comparison to the enticements of sinful language, the "pure" language of heaven pales both spiritually and aesthetically. God's language has been consciously demeaned for the convenience of aesthetic decorum. Milton refuses to let his God speak God-talk.

Stanley Fish's argument, then, that this very aesthetic vulnerability to "fallen language" (which convicts us all of our original sin) and our subsequent realization of our forbidden attraction to it (which produces a counterprocess of psycho-spiritual self-correction) is an ingenious method for preserving ethical and aesthetic equilibrium in *Paradise Lost,* but its weakness, and the weakness of all similar rationales, is its assumption that the Word of God is non-metaphorical, non-rhetorical, and eminently rational. This assumption flatly contradicts all independent evidence concerning the nature of God-talk. Specifically, it conflicts directly with what we know about the style of the most authoritative specimen of God-talk available to us — the Scriptures. Biblical language, far from being characteristically logical, straightforward, reasonable and non-metaphorical, is distinctive for just the opposite qualities: its oblique use of all the devices of metaphor, analogy, symbol and paradox. "The Holy Ghost in penning the Scriptures," wrote John Donne, "delights himself, not only with a propriety, but with a delicacy, and harmony, and melody of language; with height of Metaphors, and other figures, which may work greater impressions upon the Readers, and not with barbarous or triviall, or market, or homely language."[14] Eric Mascall, in his stimulating *Words and Images,* observes that the Bible's "typical instrument of communication is not the concept but the image, and this, as Dr. Farrer among others has pointed out,assimilates the method by which the Bible communicates truths to its readers much more to the method of the poet than to that of the metaphysician."[15] Perhaps even more convincing than the descriptive evidence that the Bible exploits a highly metaphorical style is the utilitarian argument that all God-talk, and particularly the God-talk of the Bible, of necessity *must* be metaphorical. J. F. Bethune-Baker's *Introduction to the Early History of the Christian Doctrine* contains this crucially significant passage:

> All attempts to explain the nature and relations of the Deity must largely depend on metaphor, and no one metaphor can exhaust those relations. Each metaphor can only describe one aspect of the nature of being of the Deity, and the influences which can be drawn from it have their limits when they conflict with the inferences which can be truly drawn from other metaphors describing other aspects. From one point of view Sonship is a true description of the inner relations of the Godhead: from another point of view the title *Logos* describes them best. Each metaphor must be limited by the other. The title Son may obviously imply later origin and a distinction amounting to ditheism. It is balanced by the other title *Logos,* which implies co-eternity and inseparable union. Neither title exhausts the relations. Neither may the pressed so far as to exclude the other.[16]

The language of God, and particularly the language *about* God, must be metaphorical to avoid reducing divine comment to barren mythology. The Puritan God and the Puritan language that was deemed appropriate to express Him are plausible conceptual constructs, but they present bleak models for the non-Puritan sensi-

14. *The Sermons of John Donne,* ed. George R. Potter and Evelyn M. Simpson, 10 vols. (Berkeley, 1953-62), VI, sermon 1, lines 600-5.

15. *Words and Images* (London, 1957), p. 109.

16. J. F. Bethune-Baker, *Introduction to the Early History of Christian Doctrine* (London: Methuen, n.d.), p. 160. Quoted by Ramsey, *Religious Language,* pp. 190-91.

bility. They smother all "heavenly gleams" under a stark blanket of a chilling literalism.

Bethune-Baker's argument, on the other hand, shows us the absolute necessity of avoiding the temptation to regard metaphor as anything more than a helpful tool in gaining a notion about God. No *one* metaphor can do the job, Bethune-Baker insists, and as soon as we slip from a multi-metaphorical conception of the Deity to a mono-metaphorical one, we have mythologized God, objectified Him in a gross linguistic parody of the Incarnation. Hermeneutical potential not only requires the use of metaphor, it requires its use in a carefully deliberate way.

One critical viewpoint toward *Paradise Lost* which contends that the poem exhibits a kind of language I have been calling God-talk is that of C. A. Patrides.[17] Patrides is concerned to point out that poetry and prose are radically different ways of communicating and, consequently, that *de Doctrina Christiana* is an unsuitable gloss for *Paradise Lost.* Vigorously objecting to Maurice Kelley's "calm juxtaposing of a poem with a prose treatise," he insists that because the poem is "outward looking" whereas the treatise is "inward looking," two very different kinds of expression are at work.[18] Patrides' main objection to *de Doctrina,* which he considers a "gross expedition into theology," is that its language lacks appropriate "oddness" and does not exhibit the peculiar logical behavior of genuine theological language. In *Paradise Lost,* Patrides feels, Milton "burst his limitations as a theologian"[19] and used the kind of metaphorical language appropriate for religious expression. The theological problems of *de Doctrina,* having accrued through inadequate deployment of metaphor, were resolved by Milton in *Paradise Lost* by an obedience to the principles of religious language.

Patrides' indebtedness to Ian Ramsey is apparent, particularly when he contends that the "center of gravity" of the language in *Paradise Lost* is the "model."[20] He is more willing to be

17. *"Paradise Lost* and the Language of Theology," *Language and Style in Milton,* ed. Ronald Emma and John T. Shawcross (New York: Ungar, 1967, pp. 102-19.

18. *Ibid.,* p. 104.

19. *Ibid.,* p. 105.

20. *Ibid.,* p. 108.

flexible with his definition of model than Ramsey, however, con-
ceding that one could use the terms "image, symbol, emblem,
icon" or any other term, for that matter, which adequately describes the "odd behavior of a language that is always more in intention than it is in existence and constantly points to something
beyond itself."[21] Most interestingly, Patrides points out that
"when the 'model' is centrally located, it radiates outward . . . .
When the 'model' is abandoned, however, articulation about an
insight lapses into mere affirmation in the manner of *de Doctrina.*"[22] Models, it would seem from Patrides, account of them, are
the primary safeguards of hermeneutical potential. Without them,
mythology invades and mystery flees.

Patrides admits that "one could argue that Milton abandons
the model in the last two books and in the Father's justification in
Book III," but he cautions that "the interpretation of passages
isolated from their context is surely a fruitless pastime."[23] He
argues that there is an accumulative effect in *Paradise Lost* which
works to determine the "center of gravity." Ultimately, that center of gravity turns out to be God's self-justification in Book
Three, which Patrides eventually designates as the "basic model . . . designed to throw light on the whole universe of *Paradise
Lost.*"[24]

A certain vagueness pervades Patrides' account of how
models actually work in *Paradise Lost,* and many of his generali-
zations would be more satisfying if they were accompanied by
practical and extensive demonstration. Despite its understandable
tentativeness, however, the position is provocative in suggesting
how new ground might be broken in the study of Milton's style in
Paradise Lost. Most importantly, Patrides' position pays heed to
the inherent demands for decorum. In this respect, he has my fullest backing. Pursuing his lead, we are no longer limited to a single,
formal, aesthetic set of criteria for measuring the success of *Paradise Lost,* but we can expand our analysis and judgment to include
effective vocational criticism as well, vocational criticism based

21. *Ibid.*
22. *Ibid.*
23. *Ibid.*
24. *Ibid.*, p. 110.

upon how religiously charged the language of the poem in fact is.

Where do we begin? Obviously the language of *Paradise Lost* is not uniform and it would be absurd to suppose that it should exhibit a religiously charged texture at all points. We can expect, however, that if the epic exploits God-talk at all, it would be most apt to exploit it in the scenes in Heaven, particularly in the words of God Himself. Without necessarily committing ourselves to Patrides' notion that God's speeches in Book III are the poem's "center of gravity," we can at least concede that they are somewhat of an acid test for all stylistic theories of *Paradise Lost.* Here is the epic at its most vulnerable point. If we can detect God-talk here, we should be immensely encouraged to seek it elsewhere in the epic.

Attitudes toward Milton's God usually fall into two broad categories: those concerned with His *literary* propriety and those concerned with His *religious* propriety. It is easier to justify Milton's God from a literary point of view because the defense has more room in which to maneuver; the only thing that really has to be demonstrated is that God's speeches square, more or less, with the decorum of the language elsewhere in the poem. Peter Berek, for example, can point out that "the particularly stark and 'unpoetic' expositions of doctrine in the opening episodes of Book III give the fit audience of *Paradise Lost* standards for the use of language indispensable for the proper response to the more immediately attractive parts of the poem."[25] God's language, in other words, is defended not so much on the grounds that that is the way God does in fact speak, but on the grounds that that is the way God *ought* to speak for the sake of keeping stylistic values straight in the poem. The same logic underlies Arnold Stein's apology for God's language: "The grand style would be presumptuous, and what Milton aims at is a particular kind of bare language that will rise above the familiar associations of such bareness with austerity and harshness."[26] Although the word "presumptuous" suggests some respect paid to a higher decorum than the

25. " 'Plain' and 'Ornate' Styles and the Structure of *Paradise Lost*," *PMLA*, LXXXV (March 1970), 237.

26. *Answerable Style* (Minneapolis, Minn.: University of Minnesota Press, 1953), p. 101.

mere literary, in Stein's account we still see God's language treated as a strategic inevitability rather than a value in itself. Even Irene Samuel's reasoning that "the omniscient voice of the omnipotent moral law speaks simply what is"[27] turns the matter of the Word of God into a metaphysical Q.E.D. "God," according to Miss Samuel's statement, is not more than a formal concept; there is no sense of the holy such as an ultimate personal presence or even absence would inspire. Even when such rationalizations of the starkness of God's language are supported by appeals to Puritan rhetorical standards, the argument is only partially convincing. William Haller reminds us, "We should not take too literally the boast of plainness in the sermons of the spiritual preachers. . . . a plain style did not mean for them a colorless or prosaic style."[28]

Sometimes the defense of God's language as "pure" of all rhetoric and metaphor strains quite noticeably to make its point. Fish, for example, after explaining that "in the seventeenth century . . . metaphorical and affective language are rejected in favor of the objective style of Baconian empiricism and the plain style of Puritan preaching, " insists that God's speeches are not "deficient in poetical force" because "in the context of contemporary attitudes . . . the reader's response to a rhetorical pattern like this would be emotional, even visceral, as well as intellectual." Fish sums up with this statement: "In other words, the prevailing orthodoxies — linguistic, theological, scientific — make possible an affective response to a presentation *because* it is determinedly non-affective."[29]

At best, these arguments which defend God's language on the basis of internal, *literary* propriety imply a narrow parochial appeal for the epic. They tend to leave those who are not particularly sympathetic to Puritan austerity sharing Broadbent's opinion of the divine monologue: "It had been done much better, in the Bible and the Metaphysicals, and has been done since, usually relying on Dantesque imagery and human experience."[30]

27. "The Dialogue in Heaven: A Reconsideration of *Paradise Lost,* III, 1-417," *PMLA,* LXXII (September 1957), 603.
28. Haller, p. 132.
29. Fish, pp. 61-62.
30. J. B. Broadbent, "Milton's Heaven," *Milton's Epic Poetry,* p. 144.

Can God's language in Book Three be defended on *religious* grounds? A statement that sets a reasonable standard for appropriate religious language comes from Milton himself: ". . . when we speak of knowing God it must be understood with reference to the imperfect comprehension of man, for to know God as he really is far transcends the powers of man's thoughts, much more of perception. God therefore has made as full a revelation of himself as our minds can conceive or the weakness of our nature can bear."[31] Milton's position is dictated by religious rather than literary principles of decorum, and it helps us to understand the caution with which a linguistically-minded theologian such as Ian Ramsey attacks the same problem of articulating about God: "Let us always be cautious of talking about God in straightforward language. Let us never talk as if we had privileged access to the diaries of God's private life, or expert insight into his descriptive psychology so that we may say quite cheerfully why God did what, when and where."[32]

The religious view of appropriate divine language seems to be at odds with the literary. Where the one urges a literal, straightforward, non-metaphorical God-talk, the other reflects the opinion of Geddes MacGregor who insists that "our natural intellection of God is easier for us when God's wisdom and goodness do not directly confront us (for then, like Moses, we should have to turn away our dazzled eyes, and should apprehend nothing), but are obscured and seen in the dim and distorted mirror of the wisdom and goodness we know. We do not thus know God quidditatively. We can say no more than that we know him analogically."[33] All religious counsel on the matter points to the necessary obliqueness of God-talk, which, after all, is the very hallmark of Scripture itself.

The matter, then, is clear. We test the hermeneutical potential of Book Three by measuring the quantity and quality of its God-talk. Certain characteristics of God-talk are particularly relevant to Book Three, and it may be helpful to recall them briefly. First of all, we remember, God-talk distinguishes itself by its

31. *Of Christian Doctrine,* II, ii.
32. *Religious Language* (New York: Macmillan, 1963), p. 104.
33. *Aesthetic Experience in Religion* (London: Macmillan, 1947), p. 137.

semantic dependence on the word "God." I have pointed out how "God" words have the power to wrench otherwise *ethically*-based contexts into striking *theological* significance by their mere presence. I have also tried to emphasize that because of the analogical nature of God-talk it should never be read literally. Finally, I have persistently stressed God-talk's reliance on logical impropriety as a way of calling attention to the uniqueness of its mode of communicating. Not only does God-talk exploit the familiar Christian paradox to the fullest, but it also sponsors strange, idiosyncratic collocations which often result from deliberate paratactical manipulation. Crystal points out, for example, that "what makes religious English so different [from other forms of English] is the way in which the expected collocability of one item is very often completely reversed from that expected in normal usage. For example, the term *death* in all varieties but this one has fairly predictable collocates. Here, however, the collocation is with *precious,* which superficially seems paradoxical, until placed within a theological perspective."[34]

Another important feature of God-talk, which I have not previously emphasized, is that it tends to contain a high proportion of unspecific words, words to which a uniformity of reponse is largely absent. Words such as "reverent," "profound," "devotion," and "admiration" have no predictable denotation for all people. What one person may take one of these words to mean may be quite different from what another understands. Seymour Chatman professes to find a syntactical vagueness in Milton's use of participles which corresponds functionally with the deliberately vague diction of God-talk. "So much do Milton's past participles reiterate God's infinite control at the most subliminal level of grammar," Chatman observes, "that their stylistic power is hard to ignore. *The Fruit of that Forbidden Tree* — who forbade it? *The chosen seed* — who chose it? *Satan lay vanquisht / Confounded though immortal* — who vanquished and confounded him? God, of course."[35] Grammar reinforces the semantic tyranny of the

34. "The Language of Religion," *Investigating English Style*, ed. David Crystal and Derek Davy, English Language Series, gen. ed. Randolph Quirk (London: Longmans, Green, 1967), p. 168.

35. "Milton's Participial Style," *PMLA*, LXXXIII (October, 1968), 1398.

word "God" in order, once again, to wrench an ethically-based model into theological significance.

These, then, are the linguistic phenomena which we should be on the look out for in Book Three of *Paradise Lost* if we can find any claim at all that it possesses hermeneutical potential. The potency of Milton's God-talk, in other words, is the measure of his resistance to the mythologizing pressures of epic convention against the stylistic openness which is the *sine qua non* of genuinely religious discourse. What analysis shows, to be bluntly anticipatory, is that the style of Book Three appears to descend, reluctantly, from an unquestionably high level of God-talk in the opening invocation, through a level in which that God-talk undergoes readily evident deterioration, finally to settle on a plane of total surrender to epic mythology in God's monologue. These three levels of style can be divided for the sake of analytical convenience as follows: 1) the Invocation (lines 1-55); 2) a passage of transitional description (lines 56-79); and 3) God's speech itself.

Let us begin with the Invocation. In the Invocation the word "God" appears directly only two times, and in each case its mystery is preserved by its refusal to take predication the way conventional proper nouns do. For example, in neither the phrase "God is Light" (III, 3) nor "the voice / Of God" (III, 9-10) would it be possible to substitute a conventional proper name without draining both contexts of their unique "numinal" significance. Even "Julius Caesar is Light," descriptively striking as it may be in suggesting the heroic, sagacious magnitude of Rome's Emperor, imports something quite different from what the Christian comprehends in "God is Light." Similarly, the "voice / Of God," as a performatory and creative voice (it calls for the miracle of light), has been properly qualified in context to assure its distinctiveness from any human voice.

The most significant of the *indirect* references to God in the Invocation is the phrase "bright essence increate" which exhibits more than sufficient logical impropriety to qualify as genuine God-talk. Uncreated essence, "bright" *or* dim, takes the mind far beyond the limits of conceptualization and invests the description with a religiously appropriate fund of wonder and mystery. We will have occasion to return to the Invocation when we test it for other characteristics of God-talk. For the present, however, even a cursory examination of its language discloses its complete semantic dependence upon the word "God," a key religious word which subjugates all others to the rules of its language-game.

When we move to the second level of language in Book Three, the descriptive passage which sets the scene for God's utterances, we find that the uniqueness of the word "God" has been compromised. It no longer seems to resist predicative comparison with conventional proper nouns. God is pictorialized, reduced to scale. An anthropomorphic patterning has set in: God is now a king ruling on a throne. Obviously, Milton has provided us with a model, and the issue is whether that model is "scale" or "analogue,"[36] replica or isomorph, "myth" or metaphor.

For God-talk to contain hermeneutical potential, it must retain its duality; its ability to evoke discernments depends upon an empirical anchorage which it can exploit for non-empirical insights. God-talk functions only within the overlap of metaphorical contexts, and to strip away one of those contexts is to strip away also the metaphorical "depth" which God-talk strives to release in its utterances. The descriptive passage under consideration here seriously threatens to take away God-talk's double base. The dramatic setting requires a "naturalized" God who conceptually fits into the *mise en scène.* G. B. Shaw once quipped that in Heaven an angel is no one in particular. Precisely! If we, the readers of *Paradise Lost,* are made inhabitants of Heaven (even on visitor's status) God becomes for us no one in particular, for what we have done is to take away the special mystery of God which, in fact, supports His status as an improper noun. The passage threatens to make God a super-man, an act tantamount to that described in Donne's lament: "Loth to go up the hill, or labor thus / To go to heaven, we make heaven come to us."

36. I use the terminology of Max Black (*Models and Metaphor* [Ithaca: Cornell University Press, 1962]): "In making scale models our purpose is to reproduce, in a relatively manipulable or accessible embodiment, selected features of the 'original': we want to see how the new house will look, or to find out how the airplane will fly, or to learn how the chromosome changes occur. We try to bring the remote and the unknown to our own level of middle-sized existence" (p. 221). "An analogue object is some material object, system, or process designed to reproduce as faithfully as possible in some new medium the *structure* or web of relationship in an original" (p. 222).

True, I have been assuming that Milton has drawn his model to scale and, therefore, has left us with a dramatic rigidity, a tightly-caulked Homeric language which promises little hospitality for the numinous. In a moment I hope to show the lengths Milton went to, in vain, to attempt to preserve the religious status of his model in this passage in the face of an ultimately overwhelming pressure to mythologize all hermeneutical potential out of it. First, I want to suggest why the mythologizing pressure is so intense even in spite of Milton's efforts to resist it. One might argue, for example, that it is the reader's responsibility to resist a mythologized interpretation of the passage, and that he do this by himself supplying the necessary counter-context to Heaven. Indeed, Satan does this continually in the epic when he compares his "fallen" wretchedness with his memory of heaven's glory. The powerful irony of Satan's predicament is brilliantly evoked by this method of overlapping contexts. Why, then, cannot the reader bring *his* "fallenness" to bear on the scene in heaven and thereby provide the "duality" through which God-talk can properly function? The objection, I think, is the degree of burden this places on the reader. He would be asked to maintain a stenuously critical stance in the face of the overwhelming invitation of the epic to lose himself in its drama, a request, as Peter Berek ironically suggests, which only a harried Ph.D. candidate might seriously entertain.

It is not all that bad, however, for the descriptive passage is semantically, as well as narratively, transitional. Some vestiges of God-talk do persist, which at least suggests that Milton only reluctantly succumbed to the out and out mythologizing of the third level. Milton uses a basic model of magisterial authority to present God. He "sits / High Thron'd" (III, 58), condescends in a kingly manner to bend "down his eye" (III, 58) to view the Creation, and is surrounded by "all the sanctities of Heaven" (III, 60). There is not much to distinguish him from Henry VIII except for a few tentative qualifications to the model which are genuinely religious but too few and too weak. God's throne, for instance, is "above all highth" (III, 58). This is clearly not a pictorial embellishment. Its function is to avert a too literal interpretation. Milton seems to be trying to tell his reader, "This is only a *model* of God I give you, and not even a scale model at that." The phrase is a genuine logical impropriety.

Another example occurs in the very next line where it is explained that God "bent down his eye" in order to view "His own works and their works at once" (III, 59). Here again is a splendid example of the religious qualification of a model in that the words "at once" create a provocative and creative ambiguity which invites a disclosure of God's real nature: does "at once" mean God sees two separate "works" simultaneously, or does it mean that "His own works and their works" are indeed identical? Only a hopeless literalist would want to choose one over the other because, in fact, what is being communicated in the line is not information, but disclosure.

Unfortunately, these fine examples of God-talk amount to a mere holding action in the face of the increasing demands of epic formality. The model of kingship simply overpowers the too small voice of the qualifiers, and God strides out at us from the hazy light of the Invocation with the increasing and frightening clarity of an epic hero.

There is little ambiguity in God's actual utterances in Book Three. The course and justification of divine action is explained only too clearly. Stanley Fish described God's words as "a philosophically accurate vocabulary admitting neither ambiguity or redundancy," and then goes on to remark that "God's personal character is established through his language which is conspicuously biblical and assures conviction by virtue of its references to scriptural passages every reader knows." It is probably misleading to imply, as Fish seems to, that the mere presence of biblical quotations assures a consonance with biblical style. Fish points out that there are "eight biblical sources for lines 85-86 alone."[37] The fact is that God's speech in Book Three and God's speeches as they generally appear in the Bible are quite distinct from each other in that the scriptural God rarely, if ever, supplies motives for His action whereas Milton's God, as most critics would agree, saturates His disclosure with self-justification.[38] This is an important point concerning the semantic control of "God" over the entire linguistic context because the *absence* of motive in God's biblical

37. Fish, p. 74. The original observation is contained in James Sims, *The Bible in Milton's Epics* (Florida, 1962), p. 262.

38. See Erich Auerbach, *Mimesis* (Garden City, N.Y.: Anchor, 1957), p. 8.

speeches is precisely that which lends them mystery, their hermeneutical potential. Milton, the apologete, however, is too intent
upon *clearing up* the mystery. He must have God *explain* the
"whys" and, since his God is really a mere magisterial model, the
explanations evoke neither religious nor even aesthetic satisfaction, but conjure up instead a picture of a potentate who is not
very sure of his ground.

Most of us can share Northrop Frye's ambivalence about
God's monologue: reading it as a student he thought it was "gro-
tesquely bad." After years of teaching and studying the epic he
found his "visceral reaction" to the speech still just the same, but
he could see more clearly that at first "why Milton wanted such a
speech at such a point."[39] This is precisely the problem. One's
visceral reactions demand God-talk; one's sense of logical necessity
requires conceptual language. Milton satisfies us here only conceptually. He succumbs to the literal.

He does not, however, succumb without a struggle. One of
the fascinating aspects of the opening of God's monologue is the
striking use of verbs in the future tense: ". . . desperate revenge,
that shall redound" (III, 85), ". . . false guile . . . [that] shall per-
vert" (III, 92), "Man will heark'n to his glozing lies" (III, 93).
Ostensibly Milton is merely exhibiting God's foreseeing ability. On
the other hand, the verbs display a striking sensitivity to the issue
of motives versus causes mentioned above. Waismann has noted
that "it is generally believed that an action is determined both by
causes and by motives. But if causes determine the action, no
room is left for motives, and if the motives determine the action,
no room is left for causes. Either the system of causes is complete,
then it is not possible to squeeze in a motive; or the system of
motives is complete, then it is not possible to squeeze in a
cause."[40] It is helpful to apply this principle to God's speech
because it will suggest that Milton has not been very scrupulous in
keeping motives and causes apart, particularly in the instances of
the verb phrases just cited, where motive as well as foresight is
heavily insinuated. The subtle hermeneutical potential in this in-

39. Quoted by Fish, pp. 80-1.
40. "Language Strata," *Logic and Language (Second Series),* ed. A. G. N.
Flew (Oxford: Basil Blackwell, 1966), p. 31.

teresting use of the verbs, however, is that it discloses the *one unique* instance when motive and cause can be identical — in God. In this sense the verbs evoke a genuine religious disclosure situation.

Unfortunately, the rest of the monologue simply does not live up to our hope that Milton knew what he was doing hermeneutically. As a matter of fact, his overriding concern to preserve Adam's free will involves so much conceptual justification that Milton's insistence upon it inevitably militates against any hermeneutically effective presentation of God. At any rate, these verbs at least suggest that religious disclosure is not an impossibility even in an apparently objectified dramatic situation.

To summarize the argument up to this point, the semantic control exercised by the word "God" displays a diminishing potency as Book Three progresses. While it displays great hermeneutical power in the Invocation, that power gradually declines under pressure of pictorial demands until, in God's monologue itself, it virtually disappears. The movement is very definitely from analogical to literal expression; it parallels, in fact, the epic's geographical movement from earth to Heaven. The Invocation, for example, is earthly-based. Its point of view is that of a fallen supplicant (Milton) petitioning a transcendent God for "Light" that he may "see and tell / Of things invisible to mortal sight" (III, 54-55). Two contexts are involved, creating a situation calling for some kind of analogical statement. In fact, no other kind of statement except a metaphorical one could possibly express the qualitative difference which Milton obviously acknowledges here between earth and heaven. As the point of view shifts, however, as we move geographically and descriptively into heaven itself, what was before metaphor now threatens to petrify into myth, for the insight which the metaphor presumably was to evoke is now ostensibly before us, concrete and palpable. The double vision so crucial to God-talk is no longer there. As Mrs. MacCaffrey says, "Milton's world, because it is mythical, is still a *single* world, within which metaphor, as we know it, is irrelevant."[41] The Invocation, however, is *not* part of that mythical *"single* world," and this why Professor Patrides' reference to the "throbbing metaphors of Book

41. MacCaffrey, p. 142.

III" has at least partial relevance — relevance, that is, to the Invocation.

We might ask ourselves why some metaphors in the Invocation seem to "throb" more than others. Mrs. Ferry, for instance, pays elaborate attention to the metaphors of the "Bird" (III, 38) and the "Blind" bard (III, 34-36), finding these images expressive of "the complex nature of the narrative voice — the speaker as limited human creature whose vision was dimmed by the Fall . . . and the speaker as inspired seer whose divine illumination transcends the limits of mortal vision."[42] In the sense in which she interprets these metaphors they are irrelevant in terms of God-talk. They evoke no religious insight but rather "stand in" for conceptual equivalents.

The word "light," on the other hand, partakes of a structural richness primarily because of its theological credentials, but also because it successfully coalesces the customary literal, allegorical, anagogical and tropological levels of the meaning with admirable economy. But beyond its direct metaphorical function "light" is religiously evocative because of its deliberate indefiniteness. The word discourages any conformity of response and, while this may appear a logical liability, it is quite definitely a hermeneutical asset. The denotational "play" in the word "light" tends to ward off literalism and promotes the kind of open texture which is characteristic of God-talk and which is congenial to individual discernments. Somewhat of the same effect is gained by the phrase "Won from the void and formless infinite" (III, 12). There are no formal limits to this description, and deliberately so; vagueness serves a positive function (perhaps the same function which empty space serves in Japanese landscape painting). A sense of the unexpressed, even the unexpressible, is conveyed through the deliberate obliteration of the very underpinnings of literalism: form and measurement.

In the descriptive passage after the Invocation there is some evidence of the deliberate use of unspecific words, but the attendant collocational idiosyncracies and resulting fraughtness of background seem to fade away to nothing. Milton does utilize imprecise words like "joy," "love" and "solitude," but their potency for

42. Ferry, p. 28.

hermeneutical effect is almost completely compromised by their prosaically blighting qualifiers. Exploiting "joy" and "love" as models, the best Milton can do is to qualify them weakly with adjectives that do not evoke discernments but merely suggest an increase of degree. Our fallen appreciation of "love" becomes "unrivall'd love" which we find in "blissful solitude."

Similarly, the potential "background" — the holy matrix which nourishes the biblical style — is no longer background at all once we have moved into heaven as a specifically described locale. All becomes foreground as soon as Milton seats his God upon the throne and what was in the Invocation a three-dimensional discourse structure now becomes two-dimensional, a *"single* world," in Mrs. MacCaffrey's words, "within which metaphor, as we know it, is irrelevant."

The language of Book Three, then, shows us an interesting hermeneutical regression from a fairly genuine religious style in the Invocation, through a noticeably debased religious language in the heavenly description, to a virtually complete capitulation to literal myth. Whatever the literary decorum of God's monologue, its religious decorum is suspect because it fails to evoke a proper sense of holiness.

Although I have arrived at the conclusion that Milton's God in Book Three was a hermeneutical mistake, I have at least proffered instances within Book Three where Milton's sensitivity to the behavior of God-talk was quite acute. In fact, I have suggested that Milton was only reluctantly drawn into a religiously inactive literalism by the overwhelming demands of the epic form within which he ostensibly worked. The verdict, admittedly, is not novel — few readers of *Paradise Lost* defend God's appearance in Book Three — but the criteria against which we have measured and condemned Milton's effort, I think, are. I have not looked for ways in which to justify Milton's God in terms of the internal decorum of the epic (such attempt may, if they are convincing, afford some intellectual satisfaction, but do not erase the original affront most readers instinctively feel at God's speeches), but have simply inquired if the passages depicting Him can boast any power whatever to arouse distinctively religious awareness in Christian readers. I have used the principles of God-talk as a kind of litmus test and have found Book Three's model to be opaque because it so successfully "realizes" God as an epic figure that it leaves no room for "an overplus of meaning." To quote Auerbach, Milton's account of God "runs far too smoothly. All cross-currents, all friction, all that is casual, secondary to the main events and themes, everything unresolved, truncated and uncertain, which confuses the clear progress of the action and the simple orientation, has disappeared."[43] Perhaps it was inevitable, for, as Auerbach adds, "To write history is so difficult that most historians are forced to make concessions to the technique of legend."

43. Auerbach, p. 16.

Chapter Seven: The Satanic Parable

A genuinely Christian epic ought to meet the needs of faith as well as reason, and I think *Paradise Lost* does. My conviction places me, however, in conflict with other points of view which either refuse or fail to see that faith and reason seldom co-communicate without compromise. The most serious threat to my position from this quarter is the view that understands *Paradise Lost* under an obligation to display a uniformly consistent, rational coherence, a view, in other words, that honors the needs of reason at the expense of those of faith.

Dennis Burden's *The Logical Epic* illustrates the threat well. The first sentence of that book reads, "When . . . Milton states that his argument is 'to assert Eternal Providence / And justifie the wayes of God to men' (I, 25-26), he is insisting on the rationality of his subject."[1] "The poem," he goes on a few sentences later, "is thus an exercise in clarification, finding a system and order in what could, if wrongly taken, appear to be random and inexplicable." Burden, apparently, sees a *Paradise Lost* that is a natural extension of Enlightenment thought, a theodicy in poetic regalia which, like the Enlightenment itself, might fairly be described as "fearful of all irrationalism," one which reduces "the meaning of holiness to the grandeur of the first cause of the uni-

---

1. *The Logical Epic: A Study of the Argument of Paradise Lost* (Cambridge, Mass.: Harvard University Press, 1967), p. 1. My preference is for Mrs. Ferry's less rigid understanding of the verb "justifie" in her counter-comment on I, 25-26: "To consider this opening statement in any way but as an organic poetic device, to extract it as a definitive and conclusive statement by Milton himself on the meaning of this epic would be to conceive of *Paradise Lost* as if it were a theological treatise like *Of Christian Doctrine*. Milton intended his epic to answer a question or prove a proposition only in the ways that poetry can express meanings, ways entirely different from the abstract argumentation of his treatise" (Anne Davidson Ferry, *Milton's Epic Voice: The Narrator in Paradise Lost* [Cambridge, Mass.: Harvard University Press, 1963], pp. 8-9).

verse and of morality."[2] Milton's mission, as far as Burden understands it, was one of "saving" the Bible "from apparent inconsistency and self-contradiction in order to save God from apparent
arbitrariness and absurdity."[3]

Burden's very vocabulary gives away his hostility to any
notion that *Paradise Lost* might be something more than a con-
summate specimen of reasoned argument in verse. He is primarily
attracted to the "rationality," "clarification," "system," and
"order" that he sees everywhere in the poem. His Milton comes
off as the Bible's *miglior fabbro,* a kind of supreme editor who
blue-pencils the scriptures for all that is "random and inexplicable" and thereby "saves" the biblical God from His otherwise
inherent "arbitrariness and absurdity." To state the case as simply
as possible, Burden sees a Milton who successfully eliminated from
Paradise Lost the very ingredients of a functioning God-talk. Burden's *Paradise Lost* is a steno-epic. The potential sources of religious wonder and mystery, Burden would have us believe, Milton
purged in a relentless pursuit of the logical epic.

Other critics equally committed to the principle of a logical
epic find the rationality and coherence of the poem less tidy. H.
R. Swardson, for one, examines its consistence and discovers that
"the statements and effects in the poem have no single embracing
context. There are, rather, separate insular contexts, each in an
unresolved antagonism with the other. To respond to the one we
must ignore the other."[4] The accuracy of Swardson's assessment
and his obliviousness to its religious significance strikes me as a
perfect illustration of literary criticisms's blind-spot when it comes
to interpreting Christian writing. If he finds "separate insular contexts" in *Paradise Lost* with "no single embracing context," is it
not possible — probable even — that the kind of organizing unity
he expects to find (and does not) was not the organizing unity
Milton originally intended? I agree wholeheartedly that from
Swardson's point of view *Paradise Lost* is anything but a logical

2. The characterization of the Enlightenment is Roger Shinn's ("The
Holy," *A Handbook of Christian Theology* [Cleveland and New York: Meridian, 1958], p. 169).

3. Burden, p. 4.

4. *Poetry and the Fountain of Light* (London: George Allen & Unwin,
1962), p. 146.

epic. I only suggest that there are other kinds of logic capable of providing literary coherence than the rigorously rationalistic one he exclusively honors. What Swardson condemns on the basis of apparent inconsistency with the internal decorum of the epic I applaud for quite different reasons. To my mind, Swardson's "inconsistencies" are in fact the essentials of a vital God-talk.

I should state quickly from the start that my position does not deny the patent rational structure and detail of *Paradise Lost*. My complaint against Burden, Swardson and others of their persuasion is *not* that what they say about the poem is wrong, but that in being so adamantly half-right their comments lock *Paradise Lost* into an interpretive context (language-game, if you will) which renders serious inquiry into what the epic might be trying to accomplish *religiously* irrelevant. Burden and Swardson are cousins to the Sceptic in Wisdom's parable of the Invisible Gardener.[5] They impose a language-game on the epic which effectively excludes consideration of its religious conduct, for it is a language-game that constitutionally refuses to acknowledge that such a thing as God-talk exists.

I would like to lay the foundation for an alternative language-game within which to talk about *Paradise Lost* by seriously questioning the propriety of demanding a "single embracing context" (as Swardson means the phrase) in a work which professes to be both religious in style and content. My point is that the language of faith (God-talk) is frozen out of a context that is so rationalistically-secured that no tolerance remains for the characteristic logical improprieties that enliven it. God-talk, in other words, rarely subsists in the kind of "single embracing context" that Swardson describes. It gets its coherence, as Auerbach tells us, *vertically* from God instead of *horizontally* from its "fit" with the other empirical constituents of its milieu.[6] Where "horizontal logic" sees "separate insular contexts," "vertical logic" sees a "single embracing context," and, of course, vice-versa. To insist that the communication of religious knowledge conform consistently to the dictates of horizontal logic is not only to reduce its impact and significance to human scale, but to engage in the pre-

---

5. Discussed in Chapter One.
6. *Mimesis* (New York: Anchor, 1957), p. 14.

sumptuous circularity of the argument that declares the universe rational on the grounds that if it were irrational it would not meet the demands of reason.

Horizontal *and* vertical logics are at work in *Paradise Lost*; Milton was rational *and more* when he created the poem. I firmly believe that he saw the development of a theodicy as only part of his task, that he was at least equally concerned about including conditions for genuine religious insight. This means that the "separate insular contexts," to which Swardson objects, ought not to be condemned nor even explained into unity. They should be understood instead as parables through which *Paradise Lost* makes compromise with reason and thus becomes genuinely "fraught with background."[7]

Let me try to meet the challenge of the "logical epic" head on. I choose Swardson as my adversary rather than Burden (or Waldock or John Peter, to name a few other likely candidates) because of the deliberately hostile stance he assumed toward *Paradise Lost* and because of the concise clarity with which he isolates his objections. I assume that in answering to Swardson I am answering to the critical persuasion he represents at large.

Swardson begins with a familiar critical issue. He notes a "fundamental strain, or tension" which he feels "originates in a conflict between the literary and the religious requirements Milton faced in the kind of poem he proposed."[8] He contends that the formal requirements of the epic pull against the requirements of Christian belief and, by way of example, he offers Milton's description of Mammon in Book One:

> *Mammon* led them on,
> *Mammon*, the least erected Spirit that fell
> From heav'n, for ev'n in heav'n his looks and thoughts
> Were always downward bent, admiring more
> The riches of Heav'n's pavement, trodd'n Gold,
> Then aught divine or holy else enjoy'd
> In vision beatific . . . (I, 678-84)

Swardson admits the *dramatic* success of this description. Its psychological realism promotes realistic action in the narrative.

---

7. *Ibid.*, p. 9.
8. Swardson, p. 108.

But despite its powerful "local effect," Swardson is dismayed by "what it implies about Heaven." Here are some of the questions that disturb him: "How can Mammon as an unfallen spirit show these signs of avarice? Can we picture him as one of the blessed admiring the streets of gold for their wealth? ... Isn't this a sin before Sin had entered the universe? ... What, furthermore, can gold or wealth mean to unfallen Mammon in such a situation? " and, finally, is it not a "terrible reduction of heavenly existence to picture one so high in spiritual excellence bent over musing on the worth of Heaven's pavement"? [9]

To frame a rebuttal to these questions is a challenging obligation, for they appear responsibly conceived, logical, apparently damaging to the theological integrity of the epic, and quite vexing because they seem to belie the sheer, uncomplicated delight the passage usually inspires on first reading. Frankly, in the face of them I feel like the Believer in Wisdom's parable, who stands unconvinced but helpless before the empirical evidence against his position that the Sceptic dredges up. Were I to follow the Believer's example, I would probably succumb to the Sceptic's language-game by retorting with several counter-arguments on the Sceptic's own terms. For example, must we take the admittedly "loaded" moral terms "least erected," "downward bent," "admiring more / The riches of Heav'n's pavement" necessarily as "signs of avarice"? Could not "least erected" serve as a kind of determinative phrase which sets the context for what follows? If so, can we not then see the remarks not as moral but as hierarchical judgments? As Milton points out over and over again, there are *degrees* of angel status even in their unfallenness, degrees which apparently work independently of moral categories which occur subsequent to a fall. The "least erected" angel, Mammon, is an unfallen angel of the lowest degree *not* on the basis of any avarice attached to his character, but on the basis perhaps of his *potentiality* for avarice. A similar argument is often used to justify the hints of vanity which appear in Milton's unfallen Eve. My point is that vulnerability to avaricious temptation is a personality trait rather than the moral status of Mammon at this point, a distinction which John Donne, for one, was fond of making in refer-

9. *Ibid.*, pp. 110-11.

ence to regenerate sinners: "A covetous person, who is now truly converted to God, he will exercise a spiritual covetousness still . . . So will a voluptuous man, who is turned to God, find plenty and deliciousness enough in him, to feed his soul."[10]

Finally, I might point out that it is questionable whether the admiration of Heaven's riches can be called "a sin before Sin had entered the universe," for the simple reason that admiration of riches became a sin only subsequent to the fall. Besides, it seems to me that Swardson's objection is based on the dubious notion of sin as a kind of substantial commodity that enters the universe at a certain time — that it is not and has not always been imminent. To my understanding this is a misleading distortion of the Christian dogma of sin as *actus purus,* for the purpose, I gather, of maintaining allegorical consistency at the expense of Christian insight.

Having argued thus, however, what have I accomplished? By replying to Swardson on his own rational terms have I not undermined my own position that there is a God-talk operative in *Paradise Lost* which is obedient to a logical structure all its own? To prove logical consistency in the passage through compiling debater's points seems a rather dry and humorless activity hardly appropriate to a passage that itself contains such a rare instance of Miltonic humor. A better point to begin on, I think, is the quality of our initial response, and this quality, I feel, is irrevocably determined by the attitude we bring to the passage as we read.

Swardson's attitude is that of the "serious" reader. "All I mean by 'reading seriously' is that we try to believe what he [Milton] says," he explains. "We attend to what the words mean because we want to understand what Milton means. But it is just by attending to what the words mean in their full and normal senses that we are thrown into confusion. I think that if this goes on long enough we become fatigued at the effort and decide, perhaps subconsciously, just to share Milton's irresponsibility toward language."[11] Swardson's explanation of the "serious reader"

10. *The Sermons of John Donne,* ed. George R. Potter and Evelyn M. Simpson, 10 vols. (Berkeley: University of California Press, 1953-1962), I, sermon 5, lines 14-47.

11. Swardson, p. 147.

comes as close to defining steno-reading (in Wheelwright's sense of the term[12]) as is possible and, consequently, flies in the face of Wittgenstein's principle (upon which the logic of God-talk is based) that the meaning of a word is determined by its *use*. It is inevitable that he should take as "picture" models (the Mammon episode, for example) what Milton intended to be disclosure models.[13] Instead of looking *through* the Mammon passage toward the religious discernment it was designed to arouse, Swardson looks *at* it and hence mistakes the means for the end.

My conviction is that steno-reading passages like the Mammon description in *Paradise Lost* will unquestionably lead to precisely the conclusion Swardson ultimately arrives at: that the epic, "with its gulf between official ethical lesson and the actual ethical atmosphere, is really the greatest children's poem ever written."[14] The more religiously sophisticated approach — one automatically taken by Milton's original readers — is to acknowledge that the structure of the Mammon description (and the many models similar to it in *Paradise Lost*) is the structure of the parable. When the poem's frequent "separate, insular contexts" are read as parables rather than, say, scenes, episodes, or even allegories[15], a great deal, if not all, of the "fundamental strain, or tension" that otherwise attends is relieved.

12. See Philip Wheelwright, *The Burning Fountain,* rev. ed. (Bloomington and London: Indiana University Press, 1968), pp. 14-17.

13. I borrow the distinction between "picture" and "disclosure" models from Ian Ramsey. He likens "picture" models to similes in that they share "a descriptive use in respect of some important and relevant feature of the object they model." "Disclosure" models are like metaphors because they "generate a disclosure," yield "many possibilities of articulation," are not descriptive, and do not invite explanation or paraphase. See *Models and Mystery* (London and New York: Oxford University Press, 1964), pp. 48 ff.

14. Swardson, p. 152.

15. The distinction I intend between parable and allegory is suggested by Robert Funk: "The parable does not lend itself to allegorization because parable as metaphor is designed to retain its own authority; the rationalization of its meaning tends to destroy its power as image . . . . The parable keeps the initiative in its own hand. Therein lies its hermeneutical potential" (*Language, Hermeneutic, and the Word of God* (New York: Harper and Row, 1966), p. 152.

The fundamental Christian employment of the parable is to effect an interpenetration of divine and worldly realities. Like all effective God-talk, the parable is hospitable to both horizontal and vertical (secular and sacred) logics. It is rooted resolutely in realistic, empirical soil, but it always bears with it theological qualification which more often than not appears as logical impropriety. Robert Funk, for instance, says that "like the cleverly distorted picture puzzles children used to work, the parable is a picture puzzle which prompts the question, What's wrong with this picture? Distortions of everydayness, exaggerated realism, distended concreteness, incompatible elements often subtly drawn — are what prohibit the parable from coming to us in the literal sense."[16] As a matter of fact, it is the parable's resistance to literal interpretation that gives it its unique character.

If I am right that the Mammon passage functions similarly to the parable, Swardson's reading, which I see as a "rationalizing of its meaning" that patently *does* "tend to destroy its power as image," must be judged counter to the epic's religious intention at this point, a simple case of Swardson's missing the point. My obligation, then, is to examine the passage to see what specific features of the parable it possesses in order to ascertain whether or not I am justified in urging that a parabolic, as opposed to a "steno-" reading of Mammon's description is the more appropriate to Milton's intention.

The classic definition of the parable is probably C. H. Dodd's:

> At its simplest the parable is a metaphor or simile drawn from nature or common life, arresting the hearer by its vividness or strangeness, and leaving the mind in sufficient doubt about its precise application to tease it into active thought.[17]

Four specific characteristics of the parable are clear from this definition: the parable is figurative, it possesses natural realism, it has an arresting vividness or strangeness, and it never allows itself to petrify into a single, didactic application.

Swardson's argument concedes outright several of these

16. *Ibid.*, p. 158.
17. *The Parables of the Kingdom*, rev. ed. (New York: Scribners, 1961), p. 16.

parabolic features in the Mammon passage. As a matter of fact, his major complaint is that Mammon is drawn entirely too realistically to avoid conflict with his relative perfection as an angel. Implied in Swardson's objection, of course, is that Milton's Mammon is either a simile or metaphor, drawn in human terms, for the "real" Mammon whose purity is sullied by the human model Milton imposes on him. And yet, Swardson, when it suits him, appears to ignore that Mammon's human "realism" is a metaphor. He seems to speak as though there were in fact two Mammons, a human and an angelic, both of them stumbling in and out of their appropriate language-games to do violence here to Christian dogma and there to disrupt the "single embracing context" allegedly constituting the epic's internal decorum. No wonder, then, that what a parabolic reading of the passage would see as its "vividness or strangeness" Swardson dismisses as the consequences of a fundamental incompatibility between Christian principle and epic convention.

A horizontal logician abhors strangeness because it has no place in his system; the vertical logician covets it because the system that governs him lies outside his understanding and he is always eager for new disclosures. For the one, strangeness is inconsistency; for the other, it is insight. Swardson, it appears, is committed to a horizontal logic. The vividness or strangeness of the Mammon passage is for him its incompatibility with commonsense. The pieces simply refuse to fall into place, and "strangeness" inevitably becomes synonymous with "mistake." On my own part, I find the passage hermeneutically fertile. I find the rush of provocative questions that it spawns, each one bearing its own fresh cargo of articulation possibilities, full of potential religious disclosure: How odd that Mammon, "the least erected Spirit," should be a "leader"! And the humorous word-play with "least erected" and "downward bent"! What a provocatively ambivalent blend of words denoting both status and physical description! Mammon is, of course, "least erected" both actually and figuratively, but he is perhaps more significantly "bent" physically over to admire the golden pavements at the same time that such an activity is his "bent." Even the word "riches" takes on irony from context; to think that "riches" in heaven are what the divine denizens 'trod' upon provides a richly ironic value judgment. My point is that the passage is literally alive with hermeneutical activity which the "logical" point of view simply ignores or, worse, cites as Milton's "irresponsibility toward language."[18] Mammon's description is indeed "vivid or strange" in the parabolic sense of those words, and it is this very quality which affords it a religiously salutary purposeness.

Finally, what kind of applications does the Mammon passage recommend? No specific ones, as far as I can see, but it is suggestive of an attitude that emerges from the logical oddities, the puns and the paradoxes that make up the very fabric of the description. We have, for example, all the necessary raw material for developing a Christian colloquy on riches or even a reconfirmation of the entire Christian value system. The passages also teases us with the mystery of sin (How does it occur? When does it occur? Is sin inevitable? What constitutes the committing of a sin?), but most important of all the passages applies itself to us viscerally by forcing Mammon upon our very personalities. We become Mammon through a deliberately designed identification process. Here is this angelic abstraction, laden with its impressive cargo of symbolic significance, suddenly incarnated before our eyes, and immediately the frailty of *that* flesh we see as the frailty of *our* flesh. Mammon is "arrestingly vivid" because we see ourselves in him; he is "strange" because he is simultaneously an angel caught up in the awesome drama of heavenly apostasy. Suddenly it must occur to us that the great cosmological drama of divine treason which Mammon "leads" is the identical drama that is re-enacted daily in the individual Christian's soul. Mammon brings two worlds together: the homely and the cosmic meld. Mammon's predicament is discovered as our predicament and we are suddenly stricken with the realization that it is not we who are interpreting Mammon but Mammon who is interpreting us.

Swardson's reading of the Mammon passage differs from a parabolic reading primarily in that he tends to see the elements of the segment as ends in themselves, as constituents of a narrative, rather than *means* to religious ends beyond. As parable, however, the passage can be seen as a qualified model situation — an attempt to arrange admittedly empirical detail in such a way as to create a situation capable of evoking religious discernments unat-

18. Swardson, p. 147.

tainable through discursive means. To be sure, the parabolic mode of expression necessarily forfeits the logical uniformity of the epic's "single embracing context," but it does so in order that a religious depth-dimension might develop within the chinks and fault-lines of the rational structure. The "separate insular contexts" of *Paradise Lost* are the *sine qua non* of its religious vitality; they cause the epic to be "fraught with background."

The major burden of Swardson's argument that a tension exists between the conflicting demands to Christianity and epic convention falls on his objection to what he calls the "whole martial atmosphere in the poem."[19] He feels that Milton "is concerned to emphasize the martial atmosphere even where his Christian fable does not require it." There is certainly a great deal of evidence to back this claim; the poem is full of "heroic warriors," "warlike machinery and technical military terms at every opportunity," just as Swardson says. A typical example, which he cites, is the following description of Heaven from Book Two:

> the Towr's of Heav'n are fill'd
> With Armed watch, that render all access
> Impregnable; oft on the bordering Deep
> Encamp thir Legions, or with obscure wing
> Scout far and wide into the Realm of night,
> Scorning surprise. (II, 129-34)

In addition to the fact that we find this kind of latent bellicosity in Heaven in scenes that occur even before the rebellion, Swardson objects that "it is counter to logic that Omniscience could be surprised. The Christian God cannot be surprised. To suggest that he *can* be not only violates the logic demanded by theology but it goes against the instincts given us in the usual Christian training."

My defense of Milton here is predictable. Once again I charge Swardson with pursuing a doggedly literal reading of what is really a highly-charged parabolic situation. God is not *really* capable of being surprised; He does not *really* need watchtowers or advance scouts. Milton merely exploits military models to help us appreciate Heaven's exclusivity for the righteous. Evil-doers simply do not

19. *Ibid.*, pp. 113 f.

sneak in. To assume the physical reality of armed towers in Heaven or even a figurative need for them is tantamount to asking to inspect the Salvation Army's howitzers. Milton was after much greater hermeneutical game in this passage than mere acquiescence to the formal demands of the epic.

Nevertheless, Swardson's point deserves better than that. My defense of the "whole martial atmosphere in the poem" really rests on the general propriety of military images as models to the primary theme of the entire epic. It was not the formal demands of the epic that primarily caused Milton's sabre-rattling throughout *Paradise Lost,* although epic convention certainly provided added incentive; it was the fact that his story, both religiously and narratively conceived, is about the greatest adversary situation ever: rebellion against God. The religious logic that pervades the poem down to the bedrock of its linguistic structure is that you are either *with* God or *against* Him. The most fundamental assertion that Christianity makes about sin is that it is treason. Satan is the "Adversary"; Mammon turns his back on God; we fallen readers are His enemies because we violate His will. What more appropriate set of models could there be with which to impress Christians with their status in the Christian cosmological scheme of things than models of warfare? The fact that Swardson himself says Milton plays the martial scenes "always for suspense, horror, awe, portentousness"[20] only encourages me that they indeed are powerful hermeneutical tools as Milton uses them.

My real purpose, however, for dealing with the issue of propriety of martial atmosphere in the poem is to re-open, from a different perspective, the issue of Milton's God. Swardson, predictably, condemns God for His lack of consistency. "God," he says, "is cast in two roles, one proper to the martial bustle of the epic, the other proper to the metaphysical deity of Christian theology."[21] Because I have accepted the fact of "separate insular contexts" in the poem, the notion of two Gods bothers me not a jot. As a matter of fact, the only quarrel I have with Swardson's charge is its arithmetic. I see at least three Gods in *Paradise Lost*: an epic God of martial bustle; the God of Christian Apologetics;

20. *Ibid.,* p. 124.
21. *Ibid.,* p. 116.

and *deus absconditus*, the "hidden" God of faith. All three of these Gods are vital to the evocation of a comprehensive presentation of divine awareness. The reduction of God to any single one of these mono-metaphorical roles would be to draw Him into the world and make Him, as Edwyn Bevan points out, "a part of the pattern He is alleged to create."[22] Granted, from the logical and, perhaps, from the literary point of view there is no coherence to this trinity of divine appearances in *Paradise Lost,* each one operating in its own "separate insular context." But how else could Milton have evaded the religious sterility of a God held hostage by cold logic?

The patent hermeneutical "failure" of the God of Book Three, particularly when balanced against His apologetical success, should not signal the failure of Milton's God as a whole. There we saw only one facet of the multi-metaphorical deity, the apologete of Christian dogma, necessarily rational, necessarily chilly, in order to perform adequately His appropriate function: to provide rational defenses against the potential attacks of the sceptics. In His apologetical role God is necessarily tough-minded, ethically severe and, above all, just. He has to be because as apologete He permits Himself to be answerable to the demands of human logic and human ethics. To assume, however, that Book Three in any way gives us the complete Miltonic God is to court the whole dreary history of critical complaint that Milton should never have brought the divine personality into his epic. This assumption dulls our sensitivity to the other "appearances" of God which Milton has gone to great care to engineer in the poem, appearances which complement the God of Apologetics and the God of martial bustle with a God Who is the Source of Wonder and Mystery — *deus absconditus.*

As a platform for Church Apologetics Book Three's God at least convinces us that the God who affects us religiously is *not* the God who forensically satisfies us of the ethics of His behavior. The religiously affecting God is one who guards His wonder and mystery against all conceptual efforts to freeze Him into myth. He is, in short, a God who is imperfectly known. The question before

22. *Symbolism and Belief: The Gifford Lectures 1933-1934.* (London and Glasgow: Fontana, 1962), p. 324.

us, then, is quite straightforward: Is there such a religiously-affecting awareness of an imperfectly-known God alive and well in *Paradise Lost*?

Many Christian readers find Dante's *Divine Comedy* more successful than Milton's *Paradise Lost* at projecting a sense of genuine religious sublimity. One important reason may well be what Waldock calls Dante's use of the "principle of delegated sensibility." Dante's scheme, Waldock explains, "had certain inherent advantages, not the least of which was the obliqueness that is the very key and principle of the visions. Just as the divine rays are slanted from Beatrice to Dante, coming to him by second view, so Dante himself, the figure of the poem, refracts to us the sight whether of damnation or purgation or beatitude."[23] Christianity, as a matter of fact, employs the principle of "delegated sensibility" when it sponsors the dogma of the *deus absconditus* by insisting that no knowledge of God should be sought except through Christ. The divine refraction that the Incarnate Christ accomplishes (God's revelation of Himself through the medium of man) does not cut God down to human size but opens to the human imagination His ineffable magnitude. Through oblique, delegated sensibility God is rendered with a fuller measure of religious sublimity; He is not restricted (and thereby demeaned) by the boundaries of a single metaphor.

But there is not Beatrice or Dante or even Christ (in the role of Word or revelation of God) significantly operative in *Paradise Lost*. We do have Raphael and Gabriel, of course, but what they accomplish is really a kind of *reductive* accommodation to Adam and Eve of the divine reality, literally redrawing God and His activities to human scale. The nature of Christ's appearance hardly qualifies him either as a hermeneutically-potent, delegated sensibility. What I seek in *Paradise Lost* is the source of the genuine *religious* awareness which so many readers claim to experience and which I assume to reside in some delegated sensibility in the poem. Obviously it must be a sensibility with some very specific features. First, we might expect it to be an entity that can serve as a creditable conduit between the unfallen and the fallen worlds, one,

23. *Paradise Lost and Its Critics* (Cambridge: Cambridge University Press, 1947), p. 112.

perhaps, which shares the human "fallen" perspective at the same time that it has also experienced prelapsarian bliss. It must be a sensibility that communicates a sense of wonder and mystery by evoking religious knowledge, as all religious language must, through the medium of man. In other words, it must be a sensibility which is "fallen" as we are fallen, one hounded by God as Christians are hounded, and one, nevertheless, which is aware, as Christians are aware, of the reality, the justice, and the mercy of God. I speak, of course, of Milton's Satan. He is the poem's dark Incarnation. He is the glass through which we see God darkly.

That Satan is a source of a much profounder religiosity than the juridical God that speaks in Book Three is readily apparent from a comparison of the language style each uses. Even a cursory examination reveals the ironically odd fact that Milton gives us a God in Book Three who speaks "a language and cadence . . . as unsensuous as if Milton were writing a model for the Royal Society and attempting to speak purely to the understanding,"[24] and then turns abruptly about to give us a Satan who speaks in a style that bristles with hermeneutical potential. Even critics disinterested in the peculiarities of God-talk sense the obtrusive oddness of the Satanic discourse in *Paradise Lost.* Louis Martz, for example, remarking on the language depicting Satan's first awareness of Hell (I, 56-59), reports: "It is a style that might fairly be called *tormented,* in its ambiguity and shifting syntax, in its abrupt compression. One cannot say whether 'kenn' is a verb or noun, or whether 'Angels' is a plural subject, or a possessive, either singular or plural. 'Dungeon horrible' at first may seem to be in apposition to 'dismal Situation', but the phrase then veers about to become, perhaps, the subject of the verb 'flam'd — or is 'flam'd' perhaps a participle modifying 'Furnace'? "[25] As linguistic bounty-hunters in pursuit of the fugitive religious style could we ask for a more helpfully accurate description? Or take, as another example, Stanley Fish's remark: "The fallen angels are not altogether unaware of their linguistic problem. Some words and phrases are too obviously out of place if the pretence of a rational

24. Arnold Stein, *Answerable Style* (Minneapolis: University of Minnesota Press, 1953), p. 128.

25. *The Paradise Within* (New Haven: Yale University Press, 1964), p. 119.

society is to be kept up. God, for example, is likely to be a difficult word to utter."[26] Fish, of course, wants to maintain that the
divine linguistic norm is the language of pure reason and that
Satan's fall is reflected in an irrational resort "to circumlocutions
and diabolical euphemisms," but would not the moral insinuations
that he makes towards Satan's linguistic behavior have to be insinuated even more strongly at the Bible? The Bible too finds God
a "difficult word to utter," and the logical improprieties of biblical language certainly reveal abundant instances where "some
words and phrases are too obviously out of place if the pretence of
a rational society is to be kept up."

My point is that the *literary* view — that Satan's language fits
the internal decorum of *Paradise Lost* by exhibiting a kind of
moral-linguistic depravity — simply does not square with a *religious*
account of the matter. The ideal rationality of God's discourse is
religiously sterile; it is a human, metaphysical construct that finds
its model in scholasticism. The hermeneutically affective language
of Satan, on the other hand, has the stylistic backing of the Bible
itself, which strongly suggests that Milton's purpose in developing
it was to exploit Satan as a vehicle for religious insight.

Hermeneutically potent as the texture of Satan's language
is, he is even more effective as a delegated sensibility by virtue of
the parabolic situations in which Milton places him. The situations
I have in mind are not the blatantly fantastic, allegorical produc-
tion of the war in Heaven or Satan's family reunion with Sin and
Death. They are situations which are religiously affecting to readers because of the evocative blend of realism and vivid strangeness
that they unfailingly exhibit. Unlike the allegories, these Satanic
parables are not self-contained moral exempla; they are vignettes
which "betoken mysteries."[27] Like the Mammon passage, they
are invariably rooted in "worldly" ethical dilemmas, but by the
nature of their central character, Satan, they inevitably cause
disturbing religious dimensions to surface.[28] In these parables the
sacred interpenetrates the secular.

26. Fish, p. 97.
27. Funk, p. 145.
28. In defense of the propriety of Satan as an indirect communicator of
religious awe, I cite Rudolf Otto's contention that one of the most effective

Satan's first speech in Book One, for example, anchors him ethically, linguistically, and rhetorically, as Swardson would be the first to agree, to a context of epic heroism. He speaks nostalgically of "the Glorious Enterprise," respectfully refers to God as "the Potent Victor," and rallies his followers with a fitting air of *hybris* and *virtù:*

> What though the field be lost?
> All is not lost; the unconquerable Will,
> And study of revenge, immortal hate,
> And courage never to submit or yield:
> And what is else not to be overcome? (I, 105-109)

This is a familiar, attractive and appropriate model for Milton to use. Kept within a Christian (as opposed to a mere epic) context it is heavy with ironic potential. Granted, if we take the episode out of context, we can appreciate the power of the speech as a courageous manifesto delivered by an indomitable warrior. But why would we want to? Why would we want to forfeit the religious dimension of the speech by ignoring the model status of the situation? An admiration for Satan's "heroism" can only end in its contradiction by subsequent Christian values and, regrettably, the presumptuous conclusion that Milton created unseemly conflicts between Christian and Classic values.

But Satan is a *model* here. He is a model qualified by the ever-present reality of God's providence in the background, not to mention the seventeenth-century reader's natural commitment to the fact that Satan, willy-nilly, is evil.

More specifically, the model status of Satan as epic hero is preserved by the orderly "frame" Milton places around his speeches. This qualifying frame consists of the two epithets, "Arch-Enemy" and "Apostate Angel," which precede and follow Satan's remarks. It automatically provides theological qualification of the heroic model that Satan's words create, and places the

indirect means of giving expression to the Numinous is "the 'fearful' and horrible, and even at times the revolting and the loathesome. Inasmuch as the corresponding feelings are closely analogous to that of the *tremendum,* their outlets and means of expression may become indirect modes of expressing the specific 'numinous awe' that cannot be expressed directly" (*The Idea of the Holy* [Harmondsworth, Middlesex: Penguin, 1959], p. 77).

speech in its proper Christian perspective. The situation is not much different from the one Herbert exploits in "The Collar" where two competing value-systems collide to produce a disclosure and to mark a commitment. Satan's language follows the logic of epic heroism (a bolder analogue to Herbert's distraught speaker who follows a logic of worldly prudence), but that logic is over-turned, in the reader's mind at least, by the logic of theology which identifies Satan's posture not as heroism but as apostasy. Once again an empirical moral model (heroism) is wrenched into theological significance by a theologically-charged "key" word. In this case that key word is "Apostasy" which possesses theological potency simply because it is apostasy from God that is at issue.

What, then, is disclosed by this collision of epic and religious values, and what kind of commitment is encouraged by them? If the model of epic heroism even remotely invites mis-guided admiration for Satan by readers, why not keep him a ser-pent, a toad, or some other "safe" non-glamorous entity? Aside from the appropriateness of the epic model to the theme of trea-son and rebellion, the reason, I think, is that such a valued virtue as heroism acts as an extremely effective "straw man" when it is ultimately trumped by a competing theological value. Religious disclosure is effected by throwing a respected human virtue (heroism, love, honor, duty) against a backdrop of transcendent theological virtues so that disparities between them are not con-cealed, but revealed. Ethical heroism is trumped by religious humility, *eros* by *agape,* merit by election, and so forth. The aim of the strategy is to break the grip of tradition on the language and permit it to discover new religious meaning. The old, trusted moral values take on new meaning and new function within the theological context that God's hovering presence in the back-ground creates. As we view Satan within the frame established by "Arch-Enemy" on the one side and "Apostate Angel" on the other, we ought to be attending the entire tableau as a parable, savoring the conflicts of values between fore- and back-ground, the psychological tensions spawned by those conflicts, and the general impropriety of Satan himself within that context. In other words, we ought not to look at the Satanic hero, but at the Satanic *pre-dicament* which we, as fallen humans, of course share.

Probably the most arresting, strangely vivid, Satanic predicament in *Paradise Lost* is Satan's soliloquy in Book Four. The precision with which Milton exposes the subtleties of the anguished rebel mentality — its vacillations, its rationalization, its irrepressible flashes of honesty — certainly justifies the adjective "vivid," and an appropriate "strangeness" attends the scene not only from the uncanny accuracy with which Milton uncovers human, simultaneously with demonic, psychology, but even more from the insistent pressure we feel from within to isolate the crucial factor that separates Satan from ourselves. This is a parable of alienation, made strange by its divine backdrop that signals an incessant obligation which is incessantly rejected. The "strangeness" is that such a predicament should interminably go on. Satan, in seeming to perpetuate his hellish status, becomes himself a logical impropriety. He is a fallen sinner without hope of redemption, and his condition makes the Christian promise shine so much more preciously.

On the face of it, however, there is virtually nothing in the soliloquy that is qualitatively distinct from a human ethical predicament. If we were to imagine Satan as a man regretting a decision to leave a former position, or as a husband lamenting the rejection of his estranged wife, there would be nothing in the speech to impede such a reading. Even the apparent mystery of the acknowledgment, ". . . yet all his good prov'd ill in me, / And wrought but malice" (IV, 48), is mysterious only as the human psychology is mysterious. The kindness of the lover, when one's own love has cooled, often proves "ill." There is even more psychological realism here than in the Mammon passage, and yet we inevitably feel that there is more to the scene than a naturalistic account of an individual undergoing a personal crisis. There is a "strangeness" to it as well.

At least part of the strangeness comes from our confusion as to what separates us from Satan. The realism of the soliloquy urges us to identify with his plight, even his person, and yet the stakes involved in such an identification are enormous. We desperately search for some exemption for ourselves from this Satanic dilemma, an exemption which the parable before us oddly refuses to provide. Its abuse generates a genuine disclosure situation. Our strange discomfiture at seeing ourselves in Satan leads, as it must, to self-conviction, just as Stanley Fish describes the process over and over again in *Surprised By Sin.* And yet, we ought not to close the "open-endedness" of the parable so neatly. The soliloquy's "strangeness" is not merely its capacity to provoke self-conviction. Nor is it even in our difficulty in setting our theological status apart from Satan's. This apparent strangeness of the soliloquy is easily clarified by a specific Christian dogma that provides the sought-after exemption that the epic previously announced but here cunningly withholds: "The first sort by thir own suggestion fell, / Self-tempted, self-deprav'd: Man falls deceiv'd / By th' other first: Man therefore shall find grace, / The other none . . ." (III, 129-32). An intrusion of this comforting bit of doctrine into the beginning of Book Four would have provided the kind of forensic sanitation which abounds in its source, God's monologue, and would have effectively cleansed Satan's soliloquy of its mystery. Instead of parable we would have found a piece of deductive logic.

But Milton avoids closing this parable's open-endedness, and by so doing preserves a more profound mystery. He does not allow the carefully engineered metaphorical relationship between Satan and the reader to lapse by reminding him of his exemption. Instead, he uses this metaphorical identification to exploit a further ambiguity. He raises in the reader's mind, through the vividness of Satan's subtle psychological self-analysis, the question of how God in fact executes His decrees: is the impossibility of Satan's salvation a consequence of the decree proclaimed in Book Three, or is it a consequence of Satan's own proud recalcitrance which we as fallen men can understand and even share? "But say I could repent and could obtain / By Act of Grace my former state," Satan postulates, "how soon / Would highth recall high thoughts, how soon unsay / What feign'd submission swore" (IV, 93-96). Satan's question is open-ended indeed and constitutes a much profounder evocation of the "fallen" state than we find either in *de Doctrina* or, for that matter, in Book Three of *Paradise Lost.* Sin is no mere series of infractions, as a literal account of it might suggest; sin is, as Satan effectively discovers for us, a mystery of the profoundest sort.

Satan himself draws out the mysteriousness of sin by demonstrating its imperviousness to logic. We can assume that he is honestly trying to understand the "Pride" and "Ambition" that presumably inflicts him like a disease, because his usual malice seems to be temporarily suspended for the soliloquy. His adversary, God, is accorded flattering credentials. The sun reminds Satan of God because of its "surpassing Glory" and because "at whose sight all the Stars / Hide thir diminisht heads" (IV, 34-35). A few lines later Satan refers to God as "Heav'n's matchless King" (IV, 41). He also acknowledges God as undeserving of his apostasy because God "created what I was / In that bright eminence, and with his good / Upbraided none" (IV, 43-45). God is acclaimed an easy taskmaster, deserving of thanks, and fair in the dispensation of His love. Satan scrupulously avoids casting the slightest shadow of blame upon God for his fall, and his poignant query, "Ah wherefore! " turns up no answer that logic can afford to explain the cause of his rebellion. The careful delineation of God's impeccable qualities, far from justifying Satan's sin, only increases its irrationality. A hermeneutical hole is uncovered in the very center of Satan's essence. He is determined by a mystery.

Satan's soliloquy, then, is both "vivid" and "strange." It compels us to apply it to our own condition, and yet no specific application is insisted upon nor even recommended. The whole of it is "fraught with background" and asks not to be analyzed nor interpreted. This is the method of the parable, the method of God-talk.

The theological infiltration of Satan's soliloquy is achieved through the standard patterns of God-talk. All Satan's references to God are carefully provided with theological qualification in order to prevent literal, non-parabolic readings. In the six instances in which Satan refers to God directly in the soliloquy the theological qualification is readily apparent. In some instances a theological saturation of the passage is achieved with unusually subtle ambiguity. Take, for example, Satan's invocation to the Sun at the beginning of his speech. He likens the sun to "the God / Of this new World" (IV, 33-34), having already flatteringly described it as "with surpassing Glory crown'd" (IV, 32). At face, it appears that Milton has had his Satan ironically exploit God as a metaphor for the sun (itself a semantic subtlety suggesting his apostate inversion of priorities), but soon it becomes evident that the "metaphor" refuses to know its place and insistently asserts its irresisitible authority. The adjectival clause which follows, ". . . at whose sight all the Stars / Hide thir diminisht heads" (IV, 34-35), suddenly develops a deliberately vague reference. Does the clause modify "Sun," "God," or even "Son"? Although all syntactical signals point to "Sun" as the obvious reference, the metaphor, with its suggestion of reverential awe, pulls the attention away from the syntactical Q.E.D. and draws it toward a religious disclosure (already prepared for by the invocation to Light in Book Three) that it is really the power of God behind the mystery of the Sun which causes the stars to hide their diminished heads.

Satan employs the term "Heav'n's matchless King" (IV, 41) in reference to God. The model, "King," is qualified by "Heav'n's," which, for the reader at least, should throw the description out of the empirical arena. Satan calls God "his powerful Destiny" (IV, 58). Here God is directly assigned a name which implies the mysterious control of the universe and which effectively averts an "object" or "picture" understanding of His essence. In another instance, Satan refers to God as "Heav'n's free Love" (IV, 68) Here God is tied to an abstract model, but the model itself, "Love" is given additional qualifications by the adjectives "free" and "Heav'n's," which clearly distinguishes it as *agape* not *eros*. In line 86 Satan calls God "The Omnipotent." In reality this is an adjective with an implied noun and serves as an illustration of Seymour Chatman's observation that "it is not necessary to mention His name; He is there by grammatical fiat."[29] With appropriate parabolic open-endedness the phrase leaves it to the reader to supply the implied noun for himself: "The Omnipotent" (what?). Finally, Satan again refers to God as "Heav'n's King" (IV, 111), which is simply another example of an empirical model yoked to a theological qualifier.

The effect of this theological saturation of the soliloquy is to provide a religious third-dimension to the episode, to transform merely dramatic epic scene into a Christian parable, but I should not leave the soliloquy without pointing out one additional feature: Satan consistently throughout this soliloquy attaches to God's actions a logic of *cause* rather than a logic of *motive*. Why is this of special significance? For one thing, it powerfully underscores Satan's "fallen" status psychologically, actually, and linguistically. His "fallen" state is, above all, that of "outsider." God is

29. Chatman, 1398.

no longer a personal entity in his mind but, as the epithets Satan uses throughout the soliloquy suggest, a force. God is "Powerful Destiny" and "The Omnipotent." He is characterized not as "Adversary" (which would imply personality and approachability) but as fate. A God with motives, after all, is a personal God who can be understood theoretically according to human psychology, as a reactor to counter-motives, for instance. But Satan's condition, as he honestly reveals it even to the structure of his language, is that of a rebel without a cause. God is not his adversary but his fate. The revealing disclosure that Satan's God-talk makes possible is that his condition is totally of his own doing.

Satan, then, functions as an instrument of divine insight by providing Christians with an oblique, parabolic awareness of God's presence. Until Book Nine he is the only character with this capability. Only he has the "fallen" perspective toward God which is essential to a religiously-affective God-talk. Like a stereopticon, he creates a religious third-dimension simply by his presence in a situation. To complement the straightforward Apologetics of Book Three, Satan opens up a whole new range of religiously potent ambiguity and irony. His language is living evidence that the passage from Heaven to Hell is more than a jump from one piece of theological real estate to another; it involves too a leap from one language stratum to another. I do not mean the mere rhetorical leap from "plain" to "ornate" style, which Peter Berek shrewdly describes,[30] but a leap from one language-game to another. Waismann, we recall, said, "Change the logic [of a certain field of propositions] and the propositions will take on new meanings."[31] Precisely. Satan's words, to paraphrase Wittgenstein, find their meanings not from arbitrary denotations, but from the *context* in which they are uttered. That context, I insist, is a decidedly parabolic one. When Satan, for example, utters the word "Heaven," it contains an "overplus" of meaning because of the hellish context from which it springs. From a "fallen" tongue "Heaven" is charged with a hermeneutical potency that it could never boast

30. " 'Plain' and 'Ornate' Styles and the Structure of *Paradise Lost*," *PMLA,* LXXXV (March 1970), pp. 237-46.

31. F. Waismann, "Language Strata," *Logic and Language (Second Series),* ed. A. G. N. Flew (Oxford: Basil Blackwell, 1966), p. 21.

coming from one that is "unfallen." To Satan, "Heaven" contains a galaxy of meanings which such words as "envy," "hopelessness," "anger," "revenge," "regret" can only hint at. Satan does not describe Heaven and God for us — it would be truer to say that they describe him — but the *whole context* of Satan's theological predicament in Book Four cannot help but make the reality of God a poignantly felt experience for the Christian, howbeit delivered through a delegated sensibility.

Of the several appearances of God in *Paradise Lost,* that which filters through the shadowy person of Satan best fits Rudolf Otto's characterization of "the Numinous" and, consequently, is the most religiously affective to Christian readers. As Otto points out, the traditional methods of art for evoking the sublime aware- ness of the Numinous have been "in a noteworthy way *negative,* viz., *darkness* and *silence.* The darkness must be such as is en- hanced and made all the more perceptible by contrast with some last vestige of brightness, which it is, as it were, on the point of extinguishing; hence the 'mystical' effect begins with semi-dark- ness. . . . The semi-darkness that glimmers in vaulted halls, . . . strangely quickened by the mysterious play of half-lights, has always spoken eloquently to the soul, and the builders of temples, mosques, and churches have made full use of it."[32] To Otto's list of numinously eloquent builders I think we might legitimately add the builder of *Paradise Lost,* for he too has caused God to speak eloquently to the soul through the semi-darkness of Satan.

The hermeneutical potentiality of Satan and his followers should strongly suggest that *Paradise Lost* employs both rational and non-rational channels of communication. To serve the com- plex, seemingly contradictory, requirements of a comprehensive statement of the Christian faith it has to. A rationalistic scrutiny for logical coherence and order — a neo-Higher Criticism — is of course going to discover all sorts of camouflaged inconsistencies in the poem. *Paradise Lost* should not be held further in account than a plausible *appearance* of rational coherence, for it is also obligated to preserve sufficient elbow room for hermeneutical potential to activate. The mysterious alliance of divine justice and mercy does not accommodate richly to the narrow confines of

32. Otto, pp. 83-84.

syllogistic logic. We can satisfactorily get to God only through a variety of oblique paths. If we strive to get a sense of Him through a literary epic, we must accept the fact that "separate insular contexts" in lieu of a "single embracing context" constitute the only religiously adequate way.

Chapter Eight:
The Hazards of Semantic Idolatry

God-talk is dependent upon the close logical kinship that exists between moral and theological truths in order to communicate its unique disclosures. For example, patriotism, while it may not be precisely similar to religious faith, nevertheless possesses enough structural resemblance to it to warrant its use as a model for religious commitment. Similarly, *eros* differs decidedly from *agape,* yet there is enough analogical reference between them to permit erotic love to serve, when properly qualified, as a helpful guide suggesting the direction of one might look to seek an understanding of divine love.[1]

The challenge that religious modeling poses for the reader is that he can be easily impressed with what the model appears to *say* literally and neglect to see what it *does* theologically. God-talk often gives every appearance of rendering mere moral situations when in fact it is exploiting those situations for their effectiveness as religious models. When the technique is skillfully employed, there is always the risk that the very effectiveness with which model is drawn may so attract the religiously unattuned reader that he stalls at a penultimate level of intended insight and thus forfeits whatever revelation of religious wonder and mystery these models were originally engineered to evoke. I speak, in other words, of the hazards of semantic idolatry in which readers of religious texts mistake the means to revelation for the revelation itself. I have found such idolatry widespread in the literature about *Paradise Lost.*

A typical illustration of what I mean by semantic idolatry is A. J. A. Waldock's reading of Book Nine of *Paradise Lost* in which Adam must choose between sharing Eve's fate or maintaining his obedience to God.

According to Waldock, Milton erred in depicting this

1. A somewhat similar point is made by Ian Ramsey (*Religious Language* [London: MacMillan, 1957], pp. 49-51).

episode by presenting us with "an unbearable collision of values" because we are asked to set aside "one of the highest, and really one of the oldest, of all human values: selflessness in love . . . [for] the mere doctrine that God must be obeyed." He insinuates that Milton himself, although "not in a position to admit it," felt that Adam was doing a "worthy thing" by eating the apple and joining Eve in sin. "Against the law," Waldock adjudges, "against what is theoretically good, against God, he [Adam] deliberately asserts what is for him a higher good and pursues it." The resultant conflict, as Waldock sees it, is that "the poem asks from us, at one and the same time, two incompatible responses. It requires us, not tentatively, not half-heartedly (for there can be no place really for half-heartedness here) but with the full weight of our minds to believe that he did wrong."[2]

Waldock compiles his brief against Milton very persuasively, accusing him of permitting ethical and divine values to collide. The incompatibility of these values as they converge on Adam "is so critical," he contends, that it cannot be satisfactorily resolved by giving it the label "the typical tragic conflict." To the contrary, Waldock concludes, "The conflict here is in us: it is we who are pulled in two ways, who are denied the full-hearted response that a great tragic theme allows and compels."[3]

Waldock's assessment of the ethical implications of Adam's dilemma is unquestionably correct in every detail. His error is in failing to read a religious situation religiously. As a consequence he applies the wrong critical yardstick; he assumes that the model situation Milton has depicted is all there is, and he proceeds to deliver a literary rather than a religious critique of the circumstances. That his critical attention has been arrested at a penultimate level is clear from the language he uses: our "full-hearted response," "the typical tragic conflict," "the highest, and . . . oldest, of all human values." The implied criteria behind these phrases obviously are the literary man's concern for narrative conflict and overall consistency of ethical and aesthetic values. Because Milton appears to confuse these values, Waldock finds him a casuistic blunderer and a dramatic tyro. Never once does Waldock

2. *Paradise Lost and Its Critics* (Cambridge, 1966), pp. 55-56.
3. *Ibid.*

appear at all aware that he may have been lured into the idolatry of mistaking the moral model for the religious reality behind it. For Waldock, at least, Milton's models are opaque.

Very well, how should the scene be read? How can we determine Milton's real intention when he placed Adam in that particular dilemma? Was he simply naive about the nature of the situation in which he placed his hero, as Waldock implies, or could it be that his concern had religious dimensions far beyond the mere narrative plausibility of the moral model he was exploiting for a more profound religious insight? Some illumination comes from the fact that Adam's dilemma, which Waldock finds so disturbing, was a commonplace "case of conscience" throughout Protestant casuistry during the post-Reformation. William Perkins, generally considered the "father" of Protestant casuistry, whom Milton not only read but quoted, had this to say about the "unbearable collision of values" that Waldock sees in Adam's dilemma. After declaring that "when two commandements of the morall law are opposite in respect of us; so as we cannot doe them both at the same time; the lesser commaundement give place to the greater, and doth not bind or constraine for that instant," Perkins provides an example which, for all intents and purposes, parallels Adam's dilemma precisely: "Example, I. God commaunds one thing, & the magistrate commaundes the flat contrarie; in this case which of these commaundements is to be obeyed, Honour God, or Honour the Magistrate? the answer is, that the latter must give place to the former, and the former alone in this case must be obeyed: Act. 4.19 *Whether it be right in the sight of God to obey you rather then God, judge yee.*"[4]

Perkins' case of conscience confirms Waldock's contention that Adam's dilemma, as Milton presents it, confronts us with "an unbearable collision of values," but why must we account this Milton's mistake when it was so obviously his intention? Milton was not primarily concerned about presenting a "typical tragic conflict" nor even depicting "powerful human values" in this scene. His primary goal was much more ambitious. Out of the apparent collision of divine and human values in Adam's predicament, he

---

4. *William Perkins: 1558-1602*, ed. Thomas F. Merrill (Nieuwkoop, Holland: De Graaf, 1966), p. 11.

sought to re-create the challenge for us of Acts 4:19: "Whether it be right in the sight of God to obey you rather than God, judge ye." With the epic before us we do not need the didactic counsel of William Perkins that love and honor to God must be valued, painful as it seems, above love and honor to one's wife, because Milton places us in direct dramatic participation with Adam in the struggle. There is no question, as Waldock says, that "we are pulled in two ways" as we read the episode; Milton intended for us to be! Adam's dilemma forces us, as perhaps we cannot force ourselves, to set our values straight. It is the "more worthy" thing that Adam love and obey God than that he covet, however gallantly, Eve. To be sure, we may argue along with Waldock that God requires a morally reprehensible duty of Adam, but the point is just that. This is not primarily a *moral* but, if I may stress the distinction, a *theological* situation. The discernment engineered by Milton here precisely parallels that underlying the story of Abraham and Isaac: that the love of God must be set above all other loves — even that of wife or son.

By fixing our attention upon the potential *religious* yield of the episode rather than on its apparent moral and aesthetic implausibilies, we rise from a narrowly literary bias toward the epic to a more rewarding Christian orientation, one, incidentally, that mirrors more closely that of a typical seventeenth-century churchman than any the relatively secular critical climate of today might. I say this because the seventeenth-century reader was apt to be more sophisticated than we in the evocative possibilities of religious language simply because the prevailing Christian psychology of his day made it difficult for him not to be. If his contemporary literature is to be believed, he was perfectly comfortable with the "inherent 'duality' "[5] of religious expressions and the corresponding duality of the states of mind to which they referred. He saw nothing quaint, novel nor puzzling, for example, in John Donne's commonplace remark that "a regenerate Christian, being a *new Creature,* hath also *a new facultie of Reason:* and so believeth the Mysteries of Religion, out of another reason, then as a meere natural man, he believeth naturall and

5. The term is Crystal's, p. 167.

morall things."[6] He was capable, as we often are not, of handling the oftentimes contradictory products of his "natural" and "right" (or "rectified") reasons without the kind of dismay that Waldock seems to display. Where Waldock sees only moral dilemma, he saw religious disclosure.

The difference in logical orientation implied by the terms "right" and "natural" reason is a point I would like to dwell on for a moment because it lies close to the heart of my argument that *Paradise Lost* is an epic that was intended to be read by Christians familiar with the logical behavior of religious language. The most fundamental distinction one can point to between the right and natural reasons is that each establishes a position that it regards as "objective" by appeal to a quite different authority. When the "natural" reasoner seeks "objectivity towards the Truth,"[7] for example, he resorts ultimately to observable data which constitute his final court of appeal. The "right" reasoner, on the other hand, bases his "objectivity towards the Truth" on the authority of God's decrees and edicts. Not only does the "right" reasoner place his faith upon the "evidence of things not seen," but, according to T.F. Torrance, in specifically religious matters his "appropriate act . . . is to *avoid* using 'ordinary' objectivity."[8]

At least as far as matters of religious concern go, the "right" and the "natural" reasons cannot be said to be speaking the same language. Of course they share a superficial similarity of syntax

6. *The Sermons of John Donne,* ed. George R. Potter and Evelyn M. Simpson, 10 vols. (Berkeley, 1953-62), III, Sermon 17, lines 407-13.

7. T. F. Torrance, "Faith and Philosophy," *Hibbert Journal,* XLVII (1949), 237.

8. Torrance distinguishes two notions of "objectivity" which bear heavily upon my analyses of the key apostasy situations in *Paradise Lost.* Against the inherent logical principles of "ordinary" objectivity, he poses a "true" objectivity which is "the capacity for the mind to be confirmed to or behave appropriately before its object." Sometimes, Torrance notes, the object can be beyond the powers of ordinary categories of objectivity. Even then the mind must act appropriately toward it to be truly objective. Appropriate objectivity toward God, therefore, is an eschewal of "ordinary" objectivity for one more fitting to the circumstance, i.e., an "objectivity" which acknowledges as its norm the Word and will of God rather than empirical data. See Torrance, p. 273.

and diction in their assertions, but the semantic and even logical configurations of the discourse of each are as distinct from one another as the authorities to which they look for "objectivity towards the Truth." To borrow Ludwig Wittgenstein's useful term we might say that the "right" and "natural" reasons function within the boundaries of different "language games"[9] in which what holds as confirming evidence according to the rules of one becomes heresy or nonsense according to the rules of the other. There can never be real debate between them, only confrontation, and it is such confrontations that Milton found so religiously useful in *Paradise Lost*. I would now like to turn to two confrontations which Milton uses as religious models in the epic, which I hope will clearly illustrate the point. The first is the running debate between Abdiel and Satan in Books Five and Six; the second includes the quarrel between Adam and Eve just prior to her temptation and fall and Eve's ultimate temptation by Satan.

The very names "Abdiel" (Servant of God) and "Satan" (Adversary) anticipate a situation where two rival "language-games" might appropriately be brought into collision. This is precisely what Milton does. In a normal debate we generally adjudge one side the winner on the basis of appeal to a single set of authoritative criteria. In the Abdiel-Satan debates, however, we soon see that two sets of authoritative criteria are operative, both of which have considerable ethical and religious hold upon the Christian. Satan's speeches, for example, have a great deal to commend them from an ethical point of view. He argues, in fact, with an egalitarian fervor indistinguishable from Milton's own in the political pamphlets. Similarly, Abdiel's speeches reflect a commit-

9. Ludwig Wittgenstein, *Philosophical Investigations*, trans. G.E.M. Anscombe (New York, 1953), pp. 2-33. Wittgenstein's precise meaning of "language-game" is variously interpreted. Its application here corresponds with Wilbur Urban's similar term, "universes of discourse" (*Language and Reality* [London, 1939]). Generally, we use the term to mean a language context, understanding that the objects and methods of one language-game are different from another. We "do not try to find out how much God eats for breakfast or how much he weighs" (Warren Shibles, *Wittgenstein Language and Philosophy* [Dubuque, Ia., 1969], p. 2). Ultimately, the term "language-game" is logically dependent upon Wittgenstein's axiom that "the meaning of a word is its use in the language" (loc. cit., p. 20).

ment — a loyalty and devotion to God — with which few could find fault. The point is that each debater's position, considered independent of the other, reflects exemplary values. It is only when the two are juxtaposed in the framework of a formal debate that their mutual hostility becomes shockingly apparent and the potential religious insight within the situation is released. What, in fact, happens?

Put as baldly as possible, Abdiel's "right" reason sponsors a language-game which is governed by a "logic of obedience,"[10] that is, its fundamental premise, upon which all truth assertions are supported, is divine revelation. Accordingly, Satan's "natural" reason sponsors a language-game which is governed by a "logic of empiricism," that is, a logic which finds its truth datum in observable phenomena. Such opposing language-games possess only the appearance of mutual negotiability. In fact, there is no common ground between them. They are logically immiscible.

The empirical cast of Satan's logic is clear from the passage he delivers just before Abdiel rises to challenge him:

> Who can in reason then or right assume
> Monarchy over such as live by right
> His equals, if in power and splendor less,
> In freedom equal? or can introduce
> Law and Edict on us, who without law
> Err not? (V, 794-99)

Satan's pose, of course, is one of dispassionate, objective inquiry, but the basis of his "objectivity" (not God's will but an autonomous natural principle) provokes unbelieving dismay in Abdiel. Satan has in effect reduced God to just another empirical item in the heavenly landscape and has made Him accountable to an exterior law which apparently confers "equal freedom" on all heavenly beings. Satan's newly acknowledged "God" is "things as they are." Scientific scepticism has been born.

On Abdiel's part, Satan's words are as reasonable as a call for the repeal of the law of gravity. The logical anchorage of Ab-

---

10. The term is Frederick Ferré's (*Language, Logic, and God* [New York, 1961], p. 81). Ferré goes on to point out, in the form of a summary of T. F. Torrance's position, that "rationality in theological matters does not oppose . . . but presupposes obedience . . ." (*Ibid.*).

diel's language is equally clear in his retort:

> Shalt thou give Law to God, shalt thou dispute
> With him the points of liberty, who made
> Thee what thou art, and form'd the Pow'rs of Heav'n
> Such as he pleas'd, and circumscrib'd thir being?
> (V, 822-25)

The subliminal logics of both statements really contend over the issue of what validates a truth-claim: what we see and deduce for ourselves, or what God tells us? The thrust of Abdiel's entire rebuttal to Satan is really no rebuttal at all but rather the attempt to re-establish the priorities that Satan's empiricism has overthrown. God, Abdiel can only repeat, is not beholden to any exterior law; He is the *sine qua non.*

Satan reveals his empirical commitment even more blatantly when he challenges Abdiel's assertion that "by his Word the mighty Father made / All things, ev'n thee, . . ." (V,836-37). Unwilling to accept even this fundamental dogma, Satan remains unconvinced without "the ocular proof":

> That we were form'd then say'st thou? and the work
> Of secondary hands, by task transferr'd
> From Father to his Son? strange point and new!
>   . . . who saw
> When this creation was? remember'st thou
> Thy making, while the Maker gave thee being? (V, 853-58)

Having asked the empirical question, Satan supplies his own empirical answer:

> We know no time when we were not as now;
> Known none before us, self-begot, self-rais'd
> By our own quick'ning power . . . (V, 859-61)

The pattern of Satan's regression from "right" to "natural" reason is rather ironically capsulized by Satan himself in Book Six where he recollects for us his "progress" from religious misconception to empirical "enlightenment":

> At first I thought that Liberty and Heav'n
> To heav'nly Souls had been all one; but now
> I see that most through sloth had rather serve,
> Minist'ring Spirits, train'd up in Feast and Song. (VI, 164-67)

Satan's fall to "enlightenment" is paralleled by a fall of language.

Where "right" reason knows no double meaning to words, the advent of "natural" reasoning immediately ushers in legions of strange new connotations for old words. Where "service" originally meant the natural function of love, Satan now defines it as the inevitable consequence of sloth. Throughout *Paradise Lost* we discover Milton employing similar dualisms, persuading us that along with Satan's fall, diction falls too: "love" descends to "sloth," "obedience" stoops to "servility," "freedom" drops to "slavery."

The consistency of Satan's empirical language orientation is clear throughout the epic, and his characterization of the ensuing battle in Heaven as a contention between the "servility" of the faithful angels and the "freedom" of his own hordes is in perfect keeping here. Milton's determination to include Abdiel in the scene, however, is really what saves the hermeneutical potential of the situation, its religiously evocative power. Not Satan's argument, not Abdiel's argument, but the debate as a whole functions closely along the lines of what the philosopher Max Black calls a "memorable metaphor": one which "has the power to bring two separate domains into cognitive and emotional relation by using language directly appropriate to the one as a lens for seeing the other."[11] The individual language-games of Abdiel and Satan are indeed "separate domains" which confront one another down to their semantic structures. The debate brings these conflicting domains into "cognitive and emotional relation" by permitting key words to be shared. But the sharing is of a very special sort, for rather than initiating a détente between the two hostile domains, it maintains their logical immiscibility by forcing new denotations upon the key words. Just as God's "Golden Scepter" transmutes in Beelzebub's fallen mind to an "Iron Rod" (II, 327-28), so the meanings of theologically sensitive words change when their context is shifted from a "logic of obedience" to a "logic of empiricism."

The most volatile of the shared words in the debate is "freedom", and Milton cleverly balances the Christian sense of the word ("... that whereby we are *loosed* ... *from the bondage*

---

11. Max Black, *Models and Metaphors: Studies in Language and Philosophy* (Ithaca, 1962), p. 237.

sin . . . to the intent. . *we may serve God in love* . . ."[12] against its quite distinct counterpart, "freedom" in the sense of one's liberty *from* constraints. One freedom is characterized by the positive thrust of "to" (freedom *to* "serve God in love"), while the other implies mere negative immunity (freedom *from* divine obligation).

Predictably, the "freedom speeches" of Abdiel and Satan conflict like two poles of a paradox, and the significant feature of the debate, from the point of view of religious language, is that the resultant paradox is not resolved but forced to stand. The paradox encloses and protects the crucial mystery of the Christian faith against the blight of a demeaning literalism. Satan's understanding of freedom serves as a lens through which we gain intuitive insight into Abdiel's freedom. Because the debate makes secular non-sense, we are invited to adjust our orientation so that it will make sacred wisdom. We can do this, of course, only by supplanting our empirical objectivity with the logic of obedience.

My claim, then, that the Abdiel-Satan debates not only say but do something to our orientation toward the event is based upon the assumption that Milton's intention for including the episode was to create a characteristically religious situation capable of leading the sensitive Christian reader to a genuine religious discernment. He presents us with conflicting language systems based upon opposing logical premises and assumes that their clash will ignite the desired illuminating sparks within us.

A more systematic and aggressive exploitation of this technique takes place in the separation in Book Nine in which Eve spiritedly challenges Adam for permission to divide their labors. Despite its charming domestic verisimilitude, many critics have discovered bothersome anomalies in Milton's handling of the episode, all of which generally involve ethical propriety. John Peter, for example, wonders why Milton seems to make Adam so inept at parrying Eve's arguments. After noting that "every point [Eve] advances is lucid and persuasive − a fact which greatly enhances the demureness of her replies," he then contends that "Adam's rejoinders are deliberately made to seem inferior so that this ad-

---

12. *The Christian Doctrine, The Student's Milton,* ed. Frank Allen Patterson, rev. ed. (New York, 1933), p. 1028.

vantage will remain with her."[13]

Peter sympathizes with Adam's embarrassed reluctance to admit that he feels "doubtful" about her ability to stand alone," but he is forced to trace how this reluctance leads first to the suggestion that they should "avoid / Th'attempt itself, intended by our Foe" (IX, 294-95) and then to the embarrassingly silly argument that even a temptation that fails "asperses / The tempted with dishonor foul" (IX, 296-97). Eve's rebuttal to this is devastating: ". . . his foul esteem / Sticks no dishonor on our Front, but turns / Foul on himself" (IX, 329-31). Peter also points out Adam's blunder when he asks, "Why shouldst not thou . . . thy trial choose / With me, best witness of the Virtue tri'd" (IX, 315-17), not seeing, as she does, that the trial is then no trial at all." It is not necessary to belabor the point other than to grant Mr. Peter that Adam's ineptness here must have been deliberate on Milton's part. This is so manifestly true that we hardly balk at Peter's conclusion that Eve "holds the aces of reason" and Adam "the trumps of intuition."[14] But what a curious anomaly! Why should Milton concoct a debate that has the effect of reversing a psychological pattern that the rest of the epic has worked so hard to promote? Must we sadly document a Miltonic blunder, or should we examine, perhaps, the validity of our chosen orientation toward the conversation?

Fredson Bowers, to cite another instance, is disturbed by the abruptness with which Milton appears to have Adam "cave in" to Eve in this scene after having apparently won his case with the formidable challenge:

> Wouldst thou approve thy constancy, approve
> First thy obedience. (IX, 367-68)

"If he had stopped there," Bowers contends, "Eve could have had no answer, and we would still be innocent.... After this firm assertion of his hierarchical duty to command and she to obey, he suddenly appears to cave in"[15]: "Go; for thy stay, not free, absents thee more" (IX, 372).

13. John Peter, *A Critique of Paradise Lost* (New York and London, 1960), p. 118.

14. *Ibid.*, pp. 118-19.

15. Fredson Bowers, "Adam, Eve, and The Fall in *Paradise Lost*," *PMLA*, LXXXIV, 2 (March 1969), 270.

In addition to the objections of Peter and Bowers we might add the question of the propriety of Eve's language in the quarrel. By almost any standard, her discourse in this episode is hardly consistent with her previous speeches. A minimum of scrutiny immediately reveals that she speaks an apostate language indistinguishable from Satan's. Like Satan, for example, Eve bases her remarks upon a "sense of injur'd merit" (I, 98). Miffed at what she interprets as a rebuke to her constancy, she begins a line of argument which, if we examine its logical substructure, is totally alien to all the principles of theological objectivity we have heretofore expected of her speeches. Her remarks cleave to the authority of an autonomous virtue rather than God's will. She presses a humanistically laudable (but theologically dubious) trial of ethical virtue. Like Satan's, her language presumes a self-sufficiency inappropriate to her status. Her "objectivity towards the Truth" has shifted unaccountably to an empirical base.

Equally Satanic is the fact that her language discloses the first symptoms of semantic duality which we have seen to be a linguistic concomitant to apostasy. Most noticeably, Eve assigns to the word "freedom" a new meaning. Where before she habitually understood it to describe a state of loving obedience, now she demands "freedom" *from* the moral restraints of her lover. She speaks the proud, humanistic ethic of *Areopagitica*, clearly disavowing the "fugitive and cloistered virtue" which divine edict, up to this point, had prescribed as best for her. Eve's language-game, as we will see, is a linguistic novelty in Paradise.

These three apparent anomalies in the separation scene — that Adam, even though he is highest in intellectual endowment, argues less effectively than Eve; that Adam does not seem to behave as the Lord of Creation by "caving in" to Eve; that Eve speaks like a fallen woman before her technical lapse — nourish the nagging suspicion, as they accumulate, that perhaps the problem was not Milton's but ours in not taking a proper orientation to what occurs *theologically* in the argument. It is quite possible — even probable — that our eyes have not been stage center.

To take the second anomaly first, we must agree with Bowers that Adam seems to violate the rule of hierarchy by "caving in" to Eve but only so long as we view the situation from the narrow and incomplete point of view of hierarchy alone. My position has consistently been that *Paradise Lost* has only marginal concern with patterns of ethics, hierarchies, and social mores, and that it merely exploits these patterns as models which point to higher religious realities. The separation scene is not solely based upon the principle of hierarchy despite what Bowers and C. S. Lewis[16] contend. The theological dimension of the scene includes at least such additional considerations as the principle of Christian liberty to which Adam, at this point in the epic, is beholden. Does "authority" in a prelapsarian world function the same as it does in a fallen world? Bowers insists that it does, but is it not true that *Paradise Lost* teaches throughout the opposite? Everywhere in the epic we are shown that the significance of obedience is that it is *freely* bestowed, not demanded. God Himself states the principle:

> Not free, what proof could they have giv'n sincere
> Of true allegiance, constant Faith or Love,
> Where only what they needs must do, appear'd,
> Not what they would? (III, 103-6)

Following the logic of the parallelism of "Hee for God only, shee for God in him" (IV, 299). Eve's obedience to Adam must be equally dependent upon freedom as Adam's to God. For Adam to *force* Eve's will by making her stay, as Bowers recommends, would be to violate a fundamental principle of prelapsarian liberty. From a theological point of view, "Go; for thy stay, not free, absents thee more" (IX, 372) is not "bad doctrine" at all; it is the statement of a man whose hand has been forced by the very best of doctrines: Christian liberty.

The other two anomalies respond just as rewardingly to a proper theological perspective. Peter's impression of the argument, we remember, held Eve's to be the reasonable voice and Adam's the intuitional, an anomalous situation from any point of view. But suppose we seriously consider the logical similarity of Eve's and Satan's discourse and adopt a theological perspective toward the separation scene which recognizes its apostate configuration. Despite our "feelings" about the scene, which Peter no doubt accurately describes, we know that Eve is wrong in her intention to leave Adam and that Adam is right to want her to stay; yet, the structure and tone of the argument suggests the the opposite: "the

16. *A Preface to Paradise Lost* (New York, 1961), pp. 73-78.

reasonable" course of action is apostasy; the "unreasonable," obedience. It is as if Milton were deliberately setting form and content at cross-purposes.

The pattern should be familiar, for it is the same as Adam's dilemma and the same as the Satan-Abdiel debates. The resolution of the apparent problem should also be familiar, for it demands our acknowledgment that in the separation scene, as in all scenes of apostasy in *Paradise Lost,* two conflicting "language-games" are deliberately collocated for the purpose of wrenching us from our two-dimensional ethical posture into a three-dimensional theological perspective which provides the kind of religious insight otherwise unattainable. Let us see how these conflicting language-games are exploited specifically in Adam and Eve's quarrel.

Assuming Eve's language to be apostate in structure we might expect that, like Satan's most persuasive speeches, it will follow "natural" instead of "right" reason — that it should cleave to an empirical objectivity. Similarly, we would expect Adam's language to reflect an objectivity toward the truth which holds as its authority obedience to God. To appreciate the logical conflict that these linguistic commitments involve, we should bear in mind Torrance's axioms that "rationality in theological matters does not oppose. . . but presupposes obedience" and that "the appropriate act" in theological matters" is to *avoid* using 'ordinary' objectivity." Seen in this light, the separation scene may perhaps yield fewer "ethical" inconsistencies than supposed and may reveal the reason why Milton was determined to have Eve "appear" the more engaging in the quarrel. In short, Peter's feeling that Eve speaks reason and Adam intuition and that although "both are right . . . Adam is righter because events will prove him so," may not be "paradoxical" in quite the way he thinks. It may be the case that Adam's speeches only *seem* to be based on intuition because their logical authority is not empirical. If this is true, what we are considering is a semantic rebellion on Eve's part which prepares and foreshadows a more credible temptation and fall than otherwise might have been possible if her language had not been permitted to lapse in advance. As it is, she meets Satan on an argumentative level that is common to both. Their objectivity towards the Truth is thoroughly empirical.

In a very significant way the quarrel of Adam and Eve parallels that of Chaucer's Chaunticleer and Pertelote. Chaunticleer's logical authority (his premonitory dream of disaster) is finally overturned by the force of Pertelote's empiric and practical rebuttal: "Certes, this dreem, which ye han met to-nyght, / Cometh of the greete superfluytee / Of youre rede colera, pardee, / Which causeth folk to dreden in hir dremes / Of arwes, and of fyr with rede lemes . . ."[17] Eve, like Pertelote, finds her objectivity towards the Truth from the observation of the things around her, and Adam, like Chaunticleer, takes his from a revelation. The pattern is set from the very beginning of the argument when Eve looks about the garden and observes to Adam that "the work under our labor grows, / Luxurious by restraint; what we by day / Lop overgrown, or prune, or prop, or bind, / One night or two with wanton growth derides / Tending to wild" (IX, 208-12). There should be no question about the accuracy of her observation, since Milton, only a few lines before, clearly has told us that the "work outgrew / The hands' dispatch of two Gard'ning so wide." The empirical observation leads immediately to the pragmatic recommendation:

> Let us divide our labors, thou where choice
> Leads thee, or where most needs . . .
>   while I . . .
> In yonder Spring of Roses intermixt
> With Myrtle, find what to redress till Noon. (IX, 214-19)

and the recommendation is supported by empirical evidence of a psychological nature:

> For while so near each other thus all day
> Our task we choose, what wonder if so near
> Looks intervene and smiles, or object new
> Casual discourse draw on, which intermits
> Our day's work brought to little, though begun
> Early, and th'hour of Supper comes unearn'd. (IX, 220-25)

Not only does Eve display a new "knowingness" in this speech, which suggests some progress on the way from innocence to experience, but the practical ordering of her priorities introduces a note into Paradise which we today identify as the "Protestant work ethic." No sin has been committed; Eve's innocence has in

---

17. *Nun's Priest's Tale, The Works of Geoffrey Chaucer,* ed. F. N. Robinson, 2nd. ed. (Boston, 1957), p. 200 (VII, 2926-2930).

no way been overtly compromised, but her language, because of its empirical orientation, establishes the inevitability of things to come.

Adam is confused by the new orientation of Eve's discourse and this perhaps accounts for some of his clumsiness in dealing with it. He begins by praising her practicality, however patronizingly (it is good that women "study household good" [IX, 233] and try to promote "good works in her Husband" [IX, 234]) but the theological objectivity of his stance requires him almost immediately to set about restoring a similar theological objectivity in Eve's thinking:

> Yet not so strictly hath our Lord impos'd
> Labor, as to debar us when we need
> Refreshment . . .
> For not to irksome toil, but to delight
> He made us, and delight to Reason join'd. (IX, 235-43)

God's will, not the unruly luxuriance of Eden, should dictate human conduct, Adam feels. His theological objectivity confronts and supplants Eve's empirical objectivity. At this point the issue in Adam's mind is not separation itself, but the motive for it. He sees a perilous significance in the fact that Eve is employing as her authority for objectivity an apparent empirical necessity: the garden needs more pruning. This is why he is willing to allow Eve to go off by herself provided her motive is not horticultural necessity:

> But if much converse perhaps
> Thee satiate, to short absence I could yield. (IX, 247-48)

Under these conditions Eve's departure would not violate Adam's logic of obedience and he can freely give his consent.

The danger of Satan's imminence, however, is another consideration and, as we search Adam's speeches for theological objectivity toward this threat, we are rewarded with lines which unfortunately cause us to wince at their patronizing, unheroic tone:

> The Wife, where danger or dishonor lurks,
> Safest and seemliest by her Husband stays,
> Who guards her, or with her the worst endures. (IX, 267-69)

The rules of this language-game are much more arbitrary and much less appealing than those which we will see to govern Eve's. Nevertheless, they are the only *appropriate* rules for Edenic discourse.

This is the text against which theological objectivity measures all things. The text for empirical objectivity, as Eve's and Satan's speeches abundantly show, can be found on any page of *Areopagitica*.

What about the "unkindness" that Eve allegedly meets in Adam's initial reply to her suggestion? Does it really exist, or is Eve, like Beelzebub and Satan, looking at a golden scepter and perceiving one of iron? There is no question that Eve's speeches, like Satan's, reflect a sense "of injur'd merit." The "firmness" of her "Faith and Love," she feels, has been put in question by Adam's alleged implication that it can be "shak'n or seduc't" (IX, 287). But if we carefully examine Adam's speeches up to this point, we discover no such implication at all. To the contrary, he merely expresses the strong probability that Satan

> Watches, no doubt, with greedy hope to find
> His wish and best advantage, us asunder,
> Hopeless to circumvent us join'd, where each
> To other speedy aid might lend at need. (IX, 257-60)

Adam's emphasis is upon the *mutual* strength they share together and the *mutual* vulnerability they would risk apart. The only conceivable source for Eve's "injur'd merit" would seem to be Adam's articulation of the doctrine that the "Wife . . . Safest and seemliest by her Husband stays," and this Adam is duty-bound to recite in accordance with the logic of obedience. Eve clearly plays a new language-game, and if the rules of that game produce sentiments and principles to which we respond because, to use Peter's words, of their "quiet good sense," it is only because we share the very same rules; our authority for objectivity is empirical fact too. When Eve stands up to her husband and retorts:

> And what is Faith, Love, Virtue, unassay'd
> Alone, without exterior help sustain'd? (IX, 335-36)

our humanistic sensibilities respond. We think of the rolling phrases from *Areopagitica:*

> I cannot praise a fugitive and cloistered virtue,
> unexercised and unbreathed, that never sallies out
> and sees her adversary, but slinks out of the race
> where that immortal garland is to be run for . . .[18]

18. *Areopagitica, The Student's Milton,* ed. Frank Allen Patterson, rev. ed. (New York, 1933), p. 738.

but fail, perhaps, to consider the authority for our objectivity as we applaud.

Patiently, almost doggedly, Adam replies to Eve's harangues with: "O Woman, best are all things as the will / Of God ordain'd them" (IX, 343-44) and "Seek not temptation . . . Trial will come unsought. / Wouldst thou approve thy constancy, approve / First thy obedience" (IX, 364-68). This is the litany of obedience. Its objectivity is divine. Its reason is "right."

Adam's awkwardness in the separation scene is largely the result of Milton's strategy to force immiscible language-games into collision. Adam's apparent argumentative ineptitude is mostly just that — apparent. The claims of right reason and the claims of natural reasons are given their day on the field to battle it out with one another. Nevertheless, it is difficult to suppress the strong suspicion that even though Milton's Adam is rhetorically hampered by the logic of obedience which controls his speeches, depriving them of the winsomeness of a more humanistically-oriented discourse, nevertheless, he could have done better than he did. Peter's feeling that "Adam's rejoinders are deliberately made to seem inferior"[19] is well taken. Why did Milton give the advantage to Eve?

The answer to this nagging question is perhaps lodged in a pattern we have discovered as consistent in all the apostasy situations in *Paradise Lost* — a pattern in which deeply-felt ethical convictions of human beings are deliberately juxtaposed against theological principles which contradict them. Adam's dilemma between principles of chivalry and divine obligation, Satan's heroic manifestoes in favor of civil liberty, Eve's confident uncloistered virtue versus Adam's cautious obedience, all these conflicts seem designed to shock readers out of their secular, ethical complacencies into a realization that religious obedience, as Milton defines it in *de Doctrina*, "is that virtue whereby we propose to ourselves the will of God as the *paramount* rule of our conduct, and serve him alone" [Italics mine].[20]

But there is another reason why Milton may have found it to his advantage to make Eve's side of the quarrel seem the more attractive of the two for his readers. A linguistically and ethically

19. Peter, p. 119.
20. *The Christian Doctrine*, p. 1052.

obedient Eve would, like the Lady in *Comus* be "clad in compleat steel." Eve's linguistic chastity would more than justify the Lady's confident challenge to Comus: "Fool, do not boast. Thou canst not touch the freedom of my mind" (*Comus*, 662-63). Milton was at pains to create circumstances whereby Satan could touch the freedom of Eve's mind, but as long as she was firmly anchored to a logic of obedience this would be impossible. A linguistically chaste Eve might conceivably be bewildered by Satan's blandishments (having never heard such strange logic in Paradise before) just as Adam was apparently bewildered by hers, but, committed to disparate language-games, she and Satan could hardly be expected to affect one another persuasively. No common objectivity toward the Truth brings their dialogue into consonance.

To put it bluntly, Milton calculated for Eve a linguistic fall prior to her actual one. It was an obsolutely necessary contrivance in order to preserve the credibility of the scene under the tree, but it is a contrivance that is brilliantly and subtly camouflaged by Eve's overwhelmingly attractive humanism. As we hear her enthusiastically suing for her rights as a free individual, with all the rhetorical competence that the consummately experienced Milton can give her, we can hardly be expected to maintain in our minds simultaneously that she is nevertheless dead wrong. The very basis of her appeal for us — her self-confidence — is precisely what makes her vulnerable to Satan's tempting. Even before they meet under the tree, Eve and Satan have reached an understanding. God's arbitrary decree is no longer for either tempter or tempted the authority for objectivity toward the Truth; the new authority hangs on a branch above their heads.

Proof that Eve's language has switched from theological to empirical objectivity can be had simply by comparing her speeches before and after the quarrel with Adam. How different Eve seems even as late as Book Eight when she retires from the conversation with Adam and Raphael because "Her Husband the Relater she preferr'd / Before the Angel, and of him to ask / Chose rather" (VIII, 52-54). But perhaps even more telling than this example of obedient, willing capitulation to hierarchy is the contrast between Eve's attitude toward Eden's plenty in Book Five, where

> . . . earth's hallow'd mould,
> Of God inspir'd . . .

> . . . shall confess that here on Earth
> God hath dispenst his bounties as in Heav'n (V, 321-30)

and Book Nine, where, as we have seen, the divine *gift* of plenitude has subtly changed to an *obligation:*

> . . . the work under our labor grows,
> Luxurious by restraint; what we by day
> Lop overgrown, or prune, or prop, or bind,
> One night or two with wanton growth derides
> Tending to wild. (IX, 208-12)

Prior to the quarrel, Eve's language consistently corresponded with an appropriate theological objectivity usually manifesting itself in a relentless subordination of empirical evidence to the higher authority of God's decrees (generally transmitted to her through Adam). Indeed, Eve's first speech in the epic makes this abunduntly clear:

> O thou for whom
> And from whom I was form'd flesh of they flesh,
> And without whom am to no end, my Guide
> And Head, what thou hast said is just and right. (IV, 440-43)

Eve appears almost to revel in submission when she goes on to admit that she enjoys

> So far the happier Lot, enjoying thee
> Preeminent by so much odds, while thou
> Like consort to thyself canst nowhere find. (IV, 446-48)

This is clearly not the same girl who chafes in Book Nine at her "Guide / And Head ['s]" conviction that "The Wife . . . Safest and seemliest by her Husband stays." Something has happened to her orientation toward Truth and, consequently, her status.

It is a literal and thoroughly empirical Eve, then, who talks with Satan under the tree — an Eve highly impressionable to evidence of the senses. Her first words, in fact, express amazement at an empirical anomaly:

> What may this mean? Language of Man pronounc't
> By Tongue of Brute, and human sense exprest? (IX, 553-54)

In the succeeding two lines Milton leads Eve to create an unmistakable conflict between theological and empirical authorities:

> The first at least of these I thought deni'd

To Beasts, whom God on thir Creation-Day
Created mute to all articulate sound. (IX, 555-57)

Eve has been confronted with a test: Will she choose appearances as a guide to her understanding, or divine decrees and instructions? With Baconian *élan* she seeks an empirical explanation:

Redouble then this miracle, and say,
How cam'st thou speakable of mute, . . . (IX, 562-63)

This, of course, provides the opportunity for Satan to expound upon the magical properties of the Tree of Knowledge, a view toward the three against which Basil Willey properly cautions.[21]

Eve still maintains a certain healthy scepticism, but following an empirical lead, asks to be *shown* the evidence: "But say, where grows the Tree, from hence how far?" (IX, 617) As soon as she recognizes which tree it is, Eve's empirical orientation is momentarily challenged by the theological:

Serpent, we might have spar'd our coming hither
Fruitless to mee, though Fruit be here to excess . . .
But of this Tree we may not taste nor touch:
God so commanded, and left that Command
Sole Daughter of his Voice . . . (IX, 647-53)

The issue is once again before us: which ought to have the higher claim upon us, obedience or appearances — faith or reason? But in spite of Eve's promising recognition and acknowledgment of the tree and its prohibition, and despite Milton's insistent interjection that Eve is "yet sinless" (IX, 659), it is quite evident that her demonstrated predilection for empirical rather than theological confirmation renders the persuasiveness of Satan's propositions and demonstrations irresistible.

Satan invokes the tree as the "Mother of Science" and acknowledges its power "not only to discern / Things in thir Causes, but to trace the ways of highest Agents" (IX, 680-83). In Satan's mind of course, the reversal of the priorities between natural reason and right reason is complete. The "Mother of Science" empowers him to comprehend existence as a vast, traceable network of cause-and-effect relationships. As a matter of fact, this empirical posture permits him to subordinate the "ways of highest Agents" to scientific explanation!

21. See *The Seventh Century Background* (New York, 1953), p. 245.

Against Eve's objection that the tree has been interdicted and that the consequence of death awaits disobedience, Satan bluntly replies," . . . do not believe / Those rigid threats of Death; ye shall not Die" (IX, 684-85). For confirmation, he points to himself:

> . . . look on mee,
> Mee who have touch'd and tasted, yet both live,
> And life more perfet have attain'd than Fate
> Meant mee, by vent'ring higher than my Lot. (IX, 687-90)

Eve is the opposite of the Paduan professor Basil Willey describes, who "refused to look through Galileo's telescope" because he wished to avoid a collision between metaphysical truth and empirical fact.[22] She is predisposed to pick up the "telescope" Satan proffers and assess the situation with impeccable scientific methodology:

> Great are thy Virtues, doubtless, best of Fruits,
> Though kept from Man, and worthy to be admired.
> Whose taste, too long forborne, at first assay
> Gave elocution to the mute, and taught
> The Tongue not made for Speech to speak thy praise. (IX, 745-49)

Theological "conclusions" are arrived at through empirical methods: the fruit is "worthy to be admired" and has been "kept from Man." While the apple is certainly a fine one, and while God has indeed "kept" Mankind from eating it, the context within which these assertions are made — an empirical cause-and-effect one — makes the implications tyrannical and sinister. Even the theologically respectable concept of covenant is perversely tainted by the empirical context in which it is placed. Eve argues:

> In plain then, what forbids he but to know,
> Forbids us good, forbids us to be wise?
> Such prohibitions bind not. (IX, 758-60)

An empirical rather than a theological "good" dictates the breach of contract here, and the echo in these lines of *The Tenure of Kings and Magistrates* should once again call to our minds the absurdity of applying ethics appropriate to men to God. But this is precisely what Satan does, and Eve literally falls for it. Why?

22. *Ibid.*, p. 29.

Because Eve has been made a literalist! Her empirically-oriented mind has been tricked by a fraudulent, hypocritical and erroneous premise: that the serpent who speaks to her under the tree really *is* a serpent!

Eve's blindness, regrettably, is too often our blindness when we read religious works such as *Paradise Lost.* An ambivalent attitude toward the *function* of most religious texts keep us from experiencing evocations of truly religious mystery which anthropomorphic models normally are intended to initiate. We settle for the penultimate achievement of the artist — the model itself — rather than opening our sensibilities to that toward which the model points. The price we pay for this semantic idolatry is that sooner or later the loose threads, the inconsistencies, the breaches of decorum and the annoying conundrums, that works such as *Paradise Lost* yield when they are not read theologically, accumulate to the point where we can no longer responsibly blame Milton for them. At that time we may, hopefully, entertain the possibility that we do not know how to read God-talk as rewardingly as we might, and we might even be goaded into trying to learn.

Chapter Nine :
The Sermon as Sacrament

I have been concerned in past chapters with the conduct of
God-talk in poetic devotions and in one noteworthy Christian
epic, *Paradise Lost.* In all cases I was particularly interested to
stress how language had been pressed into religious service with a
specific charge (beyond its obvious aesthetic one) to evoke an
awareness of the divine, variously called in my discussions: a
"sense of the numinous," "hermeneutical potential," and a "sense
of the presence of God." The aim of my deliberations was to
recommend an attitude for readers of religious literature which
would permit them to see God-talk for what it is: a means for
communicating the unique "overplus of meaning" which most
Christians acknowledge to be the essence of their religious faith.
My main insistence was that God-talk and poetry reveal their
kinship most in their shared freedom from the expressive limitations that dog the more logically oriented types of discourse. One
of my most significant concerns was to emphasize that poetic
God-talk can penetrate with salutary *cognitive* significance beyond
the self-contained syllogistic prison of everyday discourse and thus
can offer the promise of revelation. The revelatory potential of
God-talk confirms man's hope that his role in the world is something "more than that of the best logician."[1]

When I come to the matter of the sermon I am under some
pains to justify my inquiry, for it would seem obvious that if any
religious literature can claim a vocational *raison d'être* and a subsequent utilitarian structure it would be the sermon. But what is the
sermon's precise vocation? What job is it charged to perform?
What results should it be expected to yield? Certainly much of
the sermon's function is teaching — what the technical vocabulary
of Homiletics renders as the *Didache.* But the essence of preaching
has also been defined by its non-didactic quality — its "proclama-

1. Libuse Lukas Miller, *In Search of Self* (Philadelphia, 1961), p. 120.

tion" or *kerygma*, and it is here where God-talk becomes particularly relevant in our approach to the sermon, for if its purpose is understood primarily as instruction or, at best, as intellectual preparation for some ensuing sacramental encounter, it obviously must traffic in conceptual language which has no need for a sense of the presence of God. That presence's evocation is reserved for the sacrament itself. On the other hand, if the sermon's vocational obligation is *itself* sacramental, bearing an obligation to precipitate divine awareness, then its dependence upon God-talk is a foregone conclusion.

My first task, therefore, will be to resolve the question of the sermon's vocation by acknowledging the presence of two conflicting homiletic positions within the Anglican Church, sacramental and non-sacramental. My second task is to select a preacher whose sermons reflect a sacramental premise and, therefore, promise rewarding examples of God-talk. As subsequent pages will indicate, John Donne must be my obvious choice.

As a rule we approach the seventeenth-century sermon as we do a document. We examine its rhetorical form, we investigate its doctrinal orthodoxy, and we look for whatever insight it might provide into the social and intellectual milieu from which it comes. The sermon, for all intents and purposes, is treated no differently from a theological treatise, an ethical handbook, or at best an oratorical artifact; we attend the composition but snub the charisma. The most serious drawback of this procedure is that it completely ignores the operation of God-talk. It not only invites, but literally dictates non-religious accounts of religious activities.

The traditional approach fails because it obliges us to regard the sermon as a static literary entity rather than, as Donne understood it, a dynamic, corporate event involving preacher, congregation and the Holy Spirit. For Donne, the sermon was no mere discourse, not even a sacred preparation for some ensuing sacramental encounter with the Holy Presence. It was a decisive confrontation of congregation and Holy Ghost taking place in time. The sermon was a sacred instance of God's reaching out for man in this world; it was nothing less than an apocalyptic event.

Such claims for the sermon hardly seem in keeping with the spirit of Anglican moderation, particularly when we consider their impact on the relatively stable sacramental basis of the Church of

England at the time.[2] We might have expected such homiletic enthusiasm from the "Puritan"[3] wing of the Church with its "tendency to 'verbalism', to suppose that words alone can express or stimulate the act of worship."[4] We must, therefore, be prepared, as we examine Donne's understanding of the nature of preaching, to jettison some of our traditional notions of his complete doctrinal congeniality with the conservative "High" Church.

The fact is that Donne's idea of what the sermon was and what it was intended to do was radically opposed to the orthodoxy of his Church party. As a preaching theorist, he was a Puritan, completely in accord with the views of Thomas Cartwright and the Puritan stronghold at Cambridge.[5] The basis of this curious alliance was a shared belief that the Word of God, when preached before a congregation by an ordained minister, constituted a real encounter with the living God speaking through a human instrument, the minister. The sermon was in effect, if not in name, a sacramental rite which was an *ipso facto* effective channel of divine grace. To understand this surprising circumstance we must become familiar with several liturgical concerns of the post-Reformation which inform not only our estimate of Donne's work, but also our appreciation of the homiletic issues which separated Puritan and Anglo-Catholic preachers of the time.

A fundamental tension existed in the early decades of the Church of England as a consequence of the repudiation of the doctrine of transubstantiation. The character of the sacraments

2. A stimulating and informative discussion of Anglican and Puritan attitudes towards the sacraments is presented by John F. H. New, *Anglican and Puritan: The Basis of their Opposition 1558-1604* (London, 1964), pp. 59-81.

3. I do not use the term "Puritan" to include sectarians, but to identify those members of the Church of England, such as Thomas Cartwright, William Perkins and others, who desired alterations in church ritual or government. My definition would general exclude those who advocated disassociation of Church from State.

4. Dom Gregory Dix, *The Shape of the Liturgy,* (London, 1949), p. 312.

5. Cartwright's views find expression in his debate with John Whitgift in the Admonition Controversy. See *The Works of John Whitgift,* ed. John Ayre, 3 vols. (Cambridge: Parker Society, 1851-53), II, passim. Richard Hooker also comments on Cartwright's position in *The Laws of Ecclesiastical Polity,* V, xxi-xxii. (London: Everyman's, 1907), II, 76-105.

underwent crucial change which threatened the corporate significance of baptism and the eucharist. What had happened was the
breakdown of the medieval notion of the sacraments as modes of
entering into the redeeming action of Christ. The focus of the
redemptive event was wrenched from the immediate partaking of
the substance of Christ's flesh and blood and thrust back into
history — to Calvary — with the result, as Dom Gregory Dix expresses it, that "since the passion is wholly in the past, the church
now can only enter into it purely mentally, by *remembering* and
imagining it."[6] What had been before a corporate and immediate
confrontation with the substantial Christ was now a symbolic act
reflecting what "takes place mentally, in the isolated secrecy of
the individual's mind."[7]

This consequence of the Reformation complicated the
Anglican attitude toward the sacraments. How were they to be
understood? How were they to be esteemed? The conservative
wing of the Church cautiously compromised with the notion that
although the sacraments were memorials, they were also events
through which one could participate with Christ by virtue of the
fact that His Presence was held to be in the sacraments spiritually
though not substantially. This solution did not do away with the
problem of corporation (the real activity of the sacraments was
still restricted to the individual's interior experience), but at least
it served to obscure it.

The residue of the problem persisted in the fact that the
redeeming power of Christ was still localized in an ecclesiastical
event which had been stripped of the full impact of a decisive and
immediate confrontation. There was an uncomfortable vagueness
about the nature of the Divine participation in this most important of Christian rites that was reflected in the endless disputes
over transsubstantiation, consubstantiation, Zwinglianism and the
like. Because of the breakdown of the corporate significance of
the sacraments and the confusion that consequently followed, the
sermon began to receive renewed attention. If the Holy Ghost
were present and operative during the administering of the Elements, why should He not be present and operative during the

6. Dix, p. 623.
7. *Ibid.*

administering of the Word, in the sermon? As a result of such thinking, the continental Reformers began to view the preached sermon as a liturgical function at least as efficacious to salvation as the sacraments themselves. Moreover, the corporate significance lost to the sacraments was regained, since the Holy Presence was not localized in wafer and wine, but sprinkled like a drizzle, as Donne was fond of expressing it, over the whole congregation as the sermon was delivered. Thus, the sermon was seen by some as a complementary mode of encounter with God which paralleled the rites of sacrament.

In England, there was understandable resistance to this innovation. The conservative Anglicans had not broken with Rome as radically as the continental Protestants had. They still cleaved obdurately to a sacramental approach to grace and esteemed the sermon as a useful, but not necessary, catechism which served to instruct the Christian on the significance of his partaking of the Elements and baptism. The general attitude was reflected in Bishop Laud's opinion that "it is *versus altare,* 'towards His altar,' as the greatest place of God's residence upon earth. (I say the greatest, yea, greater than the pulpit; for there 'tis *Hoc est corpus meum,* 'This is my body', but in the pulpit 'tis at most but *Hoc est verbum meum,* 'This is My Word.' And a greater reverence, no doubt, is due to the body than to the word of our Lord.)"[8]

Here, in fine, is the distinction between the Anglo-Catholic and Puritan points of view. The center of the Anglican worship was *corpus,* the Puritan, *verbum,* and the tension between these perspectives had enormous consequences on preaching style far above superficial rhetorical distinctions. The Puritans, following the leads of Luther and Calvin, understood "Word of God" dynamically. The Word was not mere Scripture; it was Christ, immediate and present, mediated through the Holy Spirit in the ordinance of preaching. The Holy Ghost worked as the minister preached and descended upon the congregation providing a direct confrontation with the Holy Presence. As the most influential Puritan of his day, William Perkins, insisted, "The Gospell preach-

8. William Laud, *The Works . . . ,* ed. William Scott and James Bliss, 7 vols. (Oxford: Library of Anglo-Catholic Theology, 1847-60), VI, 57.

ed is, in the flourishing estate of Christs Church, that ordinarie means to beget faith."[9]

The Anglicans, however, as Laud's statement clearly shows, held no such exalted estimation of the efficacy of the Word preached. The "body" was still the most important feature; Christian worship remained centered about the sacraments. Consequently, they placed preaching at the periphery of liturgical concern and saw no distinction between the Gospel preached and the Scripture read. The Word in any form was considered a static mode of edification, a scholarly aid to faith, but not an instance of divine activity. In short, the Anglicans "assumed the primacy of the sacramental process, and Puritanism the transcending importance of the Gospel confrontation."[10]

When we introduce John Donne into this context, we see immediately that his attitude toward preaching was anything but Anglo-Catholic. Against the insistence of Richard Hooker that "we are when we name the *word of God* always to mean the *Scripture only,"*[11] Donne pressed a radically dynamic definition: "Christ is *verbum,* The word; not A word, but The Word: The minister is *Vox,* voyce; not A voyce, but The Voyce, The voyce of that word, and no other."[12] This passage, and the many like it scattered throughout Donne's work, is pivotal to our understanding of his preaching theory; it sets him decisively separate from the other preachers of his Church party and places him in the homiletic camp of the Puritans. It means that the Word of God was not a historical revelation given to men once and for all in the past, but is continually being spoken afresh whenever the Gospel is preached. The written Word was history, but the preached Word was dynamically present because preaching drew forth the efficacious presence of the Holy Spirit into the corporate worship of the church. The Word of God was effective, in other words, only when

9. William Perkins, "The Foundation of Christian Religion Gathered into Six Principles," *The Workes of . . .* (Cambridge, 1609), I, 71.

10. New, p. 71.

11. *Laws of Ecclesiastical Polity,* V, xxi, 2.

12. *The Sermons of John Donne,* ed. George R. Potter and Evelyn M. Simpson, 10 vols. (Berkeley, 1953-62), II, 7, 304-11. Future references to Donne's sermons will be to this edition and quotations will be identified, as here, by volume, sermon and line.

it was dynamically presented to the congregation in the sermon. "Nothing is Gospell," Donne preached, "nor *Evangelium,* good message, *if it be not put into a Messengers mouth; and delivered by him"* (VII, 16, 125-27).[13]

Donne, therefore, understood "Word of God" in the fullest Protestant Reformed sense, a position that demanded a reappraisal and re-adjustment of the delicate balance between the sacraments and preaching. In terms of official statement, the Puritans and Anglicans were doctrinally at one on the issue of the sacraments, but, as John New points out, "covertly, . . . [they] were decisively separated in their views."[14] Consequently, we do not find Donne explicitly subordinating the significance of the sacramental rites to preaching. What we do find, however, is a continual declaration that preaching is of *equal* importance to salvation as Baptism and the Eucharist, an avowal which, in effect if not in word, raised preaching to the level of a sacrament. "That water," Donne preached, "which is made *equal* [italics mine] with the *preaching* of the Word . . . is onely the *Sacrament of Baptisme"* (V, 6, 638-41). The full possession of Christ by the believer, he was convinced, required more than just baptism and more than just preaching. It depended upon a trinity of ecclesiastical functions: ". . . the Gospell, and the *preaching* thereof, is as the deed that conveys *Jesus* unto us; the water, the *Baptisme,* is as the *Seale,* that assures it; and the *bloud,* the *Sacrament,* is the delivery of Christ into us" (V, 6, 687-90). The equity of salutary importance which Donne accords to preaching, baptism and the Eucharist is manifest here, and it is no surprise to find Donne referring to preaching in terms which are to all effects sacramental: "It is impossible to receive the *Sacrament of Baptisme,* except the soule have received *Sacramentum fidei,* the Sacrament of faith, that is the Word preached"' (V, 13, 614-16). So zealous was Donne to exalt preaching to a sacramental significance that he was not above noting that the "Sacraments were instituted by Christ, as subsidi-

13. Hooker was vehemently opposed to similar statements put forth by the Puritans: "But the principal cause of *writing the Gospel* [according to the Puritans] was, *that it might be preached* upon or interpreted by public ministers apt and authorized thereunto" (*Laws of Ecclesiastical Polity,* V, xxii, 7).

14. New, p. 64.

ary things, in a great part, for our infirmity, who stand in need of such visible and sensible assistances" (X, 2, 137-38).

It was not Donne's intention, however, to downgrade the sacraments; it was the sacramental quality of the sermon he wished to exalt. He no doubt recognized the sermon's potential to fill the corporate vacuum that had been left by the Reformation's dismissal of the substantial presence of Christ in the sacramental elements. At any rate, he harped on the corporate value of preaching continually throughout his sermons. On one occasion, for example, he preached, "As we have read of some Generals, in secular story, that in great Services have knighted their whole Army, So the Holy Ghost Sanctifies, and Canonizes whole Congregations" (V, 1, 661-64). Elsewhere he declared, "The Holy Ghost casts a net over the whole Congregation, in this Ordinance of preaching, and catches all that break not out" (VI, 16, 653-54), or again: "So the Holy Ghost loved the World, as that he would dwell in it, and inable men, in his Ministry, and by his gifts, to apply this mercy of the Father, and this merit of the Son, to particular souls, and to whole Congregations" (VII, 18, 87-90).

Malcolm Mackenzie Ross confirms the view I have taken in regard to the Reformation's impact on the sacraments when he states that "the separation in the minds of the Reformers of symbol from truth-as-fact was to destroy the symbolic reach of the Eucharist by reducing it from corporate and objective act to individual subjective recollection."[15] Later in his study, however, he notes with curious surprise that "it is in the thoroughly nonsacramental Calvinist phase of the Reformation that the emphasis on corporate worship is recovered."[16] This should not be surprising at all. Spiritual corporation was in fact re-achieved, at least in Puritan homiletic doctrine and in Donne's view, by means of understanding the sermon as a sacramental event.

Such an attitude toward the sermon required doctrinal underpinnings before it could be seriously put into practice. These were available in the doctrine of the continental Reformers. The

15. *Poetry and Dogma: The Transfiguration of Eucharist Symbols in Seventeenth Century English Poetry* (New Brunswick, N.J.: Rutgers University Press, 1954), p. 35.
16. *Ibid.,* p. 53.

reformers had developed their own *ex opere operato* doctrine which they applied not to the sacraments (the "visible Word") but to preaching (the "audible Word"). Traditionally, the *ex opere operato* was a doctrine which stressed the independence of the results of an operation from the acting subject so as to assert the validity of the administration of the Elements independent from the dignity and standing of the administrating clergyman. In 1562, Henry Bullinger published in his *Confessio Helvetica Posterior* an application of this principle to preaching which became common doctrine for the whole Reformation.[17] Briefly, this marriage of *ex opere operato* with preaching implied the almost certain presence of the Word of God in the mouth of the ordained minister when he preached. The *ex opere* principle, in short, lifted the sermon from the level of a mundane discourse *about* the Word to a status whereby it became the Word of God itself — God's immediate speaking to his people through the instrument of the minister ("The minister is *Vox,* voyce; not A Voyce, but The voyce, The voyce of that word, and no other"). Luther once expressed the phenomenon in words remarkably similar to Donne's: "To be sure, I do hear the sermon; however, I am wont to ask: 'Who is speaking?' The Pastor? By no means! You do not hear the pastor. Of course, the voice is his, but the words he employs are really spoken by my God."[18]

The *ex opere* principle, therefore, provided a rationale for the claim that God was dynamically present during the preaching of a sermon. The sermon event paralleled the sacramental rite; in both instances the claim was made that God's saving grace was uniquely active because the Holy Spirit was efficaciously in attendance. This explains Donne's meaning in such assertions as this: "It is not therefore the Gospell meerly, but the preaching of the Gospell, that is this spirit . . . The spirit of the Minister, is not so pure, as the spirit of God, but it is the chariot, the meanes, by which God will enter in to you" (V, 6, 561-66). Hooker, of course, had expressed his indignation at Cartwright and his group for

---

17. See Heiko A. Oberman, "Preaching and the Word in the Reformation," *Theology Today,* XVIII (1961), 16-29.

18. *Luther's Works,* ed. Jaroslav Pelikan, 55 vols. (St. Louis, Mo., 1957), XXII, 528.

asserting the same principle that "the principal cause of writing the Gospel was, *that it might be preached* upon or interpreted by public ministers apt and authorized thereunto."[19] He might as easily have leveled his charge at Donne's declaration that "this *calling,* implies a voice, as well as a Word; it is by the word; but not by the Word read at home. Though that be a pious exercise; nor by the word submitted to private interpretation; but *by the Word preached"* (VII, 5, 593-96).

Hooker, as we have seen, recognized only the static form of the Word of God: the Word meant nothing else but the Scriptures. Donne, along with the Puritans and the reformers, argued a dynamic form which took precedence over the bare written word: "Howsoever it [the Bible] be gospel in itself, it is not Gospel to us if it be not preached in the Congregation" (I, 8, 240-41).

The tension underlying these two disparate understandings of "Word of God" finally erupted in the Admonition Controversy, but our most efficient access to the issue is the *Laws of Ecclesiastical Polity* where, in Book Five, Hooker provides a concise resume of the conflict and energetically supports Whitgift against his Puritan opponent. The basic question, according to Hooker, was "whether the word of God be any *ordinary* mean to save the souls of men, in that it is either privately studied or publicly read and so made known, or else only as the same is *preached".*[20] Since Hooker had committed himself, as we have seen, to a static conception of the Word, he saw no distinction between reading and preaching. This was not sheer perverseness on his part; his attitude was a logical consequence of a Thomistic approach to the mechanics of faith which he shared with other Anglo-Catholic divines. Hooker understood faith as the result of two operations: *"apprehension* and *assent."*[21] Belief was a matter of marshalling one's reason and will into accord with revealed truth. It therefore made little difference which form that truth took so long as its authenticity was assured. The Scriptures, he felt, were unquestionably authentic and therefore he was reluctant to accord sermons a higher veracity.

19. *Laws,* V, xxii, 7.
20. *Laws,* V, xxi, 1.
21. *Laws,* V, xxii, 8.

The intellectual bias of Hooker's description of the process of faith jars with what we might call the "dialectical"[22] understanding held by the Puritans and the Reformers. The dialectical view comprehended faith as an instance when the human spirit and the Holy Spirit bore mutual witness in a direct confrontation. Donne, for example, expressed the phenomenon in this way: ". . . when the Spirit, and our spirit agree in their testimony, That he hath spoke comfortably to my soule, and my soule hath apprehended comfort by that speech, That, (to use Christ's similitude) *He hath piped, and we have danced,* He hath showed me my Saviour, and my spirit hath rejoiced in God my Saviour, He deposes for the Decree of my Election" (V, 2, 428-33). This description of election (faith) is one of dynamic encounter. It is dialogue with the Holy, not a more exercise in reasoned assent as Hooker apparently understood the process.[23] It is no wonder, then, that Hooker failed to appreciate the dynamic potentiality of the World of God and could reasonably conclude that " to this end the word of God not otherwise serveth than only in the nature of a doctrinal instrument. It saveth because it maketh 'wish to salvation.' "[24]

22. Cornelius van Til observes that "the Reformers held to conscience as the central point of man's natural self-knowledge. Through it, they said, man has knowledge of sin and of his lost condition. In conscience they saw the immanent possibility of contact for the gospel. But this immanent possibility had for them to be touched from without to turn into an actual knowledge of God. In short, the Reformers . . . held to a dialectical relationship between natural and revealed theology, natural and revealed ethics." See *The New Modernism* (Philadelphia, 1947), pp. 252-53.

23. The issue between the emphasis placed upon the individual religious experience by the Reformers and the institutional religion stressed by Hooker is explored by L. S. Thornton in *Richard Hooker: A Study of His Theology* (London, 1924), p. 81. Father Thornton contends that the Reformers' "reassertion of Augustinian teaching about grace . . . tended to make them think of God's gracious election upon man as a direct relationship of Divine to human personality, of God to individual souls; as a secret unfettered transaction of Person with person and of an equally unfettered response" (p. 81). Donne's commitment to the Reformation cause made him vulnerable to much of Father Thornton's criticism of the Reformers in general but not in regard to subordinating the paramount importance of the Church as an institution.

24. *Laws,* V, xxi, 3.

The objections that Cartwright and Donne would have raised to this statement are two. First, they would have insisted that the phrase "word of God" in this context be changed to "Scriptures" in order that both the dynamic and static modes of God's revelation be preserved. Secondly, they would have objected rigorously to Hooker's claim that the written canon ("a doctrinal instrument") could save. It was the Word read. Their fundamental conviction was, to use Oberman's phrase, that "the sermon does not inspire good inclinations — it is an apocalyptic event."[25]

But what precisely does apocalyptic event mean? It means simply that in the preaching of the Word the doors of Heaven and Hell are put in motion, that the sermon, by virtue of its *ex opere* warrant, is automatically effective. William Perkins went so far as to say that "yea, the very sound thereof beeing but once heard, is by the assistance of Gods spirit, extraordinarily effectual,"[26] meaning that the Word of God is not sent out through the ministerial instrument without drawing from those who hear, a decision. "Never deceive your own souls," Donne preached, "He, to whom Christ hath been preached, and believes not, shall be damned" (VII, 16, 175), and again, "He answers us in Preaching; but with that terrible commination, that even his work may be the saver of death unto death" (VII, 12, 866-68), and still again: "Absolution is conferred, or withheld in Preaching . . . the proposing of promises of the Gospel in Preaching, is that binding and loosing on earth, which bindes and looses in Heaven" (VII, 12, 720-28).

The sermon, to Donne, was clearly a sacred, corporate rite of the utmost salutary significance. It was an event in which God talked to man and man was expected to reply. Naturally, the bare reading of the Scriptures had to take second place to such a momentous instance of Divine confrontation. Private reading of the Bible was therefore of a lower order in the hierarchy of redemptive functions. It was useful for spiritual nourishment, but not sufficient to initiate faith. Even miracles and private inspiration had to bow before the primacy of preaching: "If Christ do appear to any man, in the power of a miracle, or in a private inspiration, yet he appears but in a weakness, as in infancy, till he

25. Oberman, p. 18.
26. Perkins, I, 71.

speak, till he bring a man to the hearing of his voice, in a setled Church, and in the Ordinance of preaching" (VII, 5, 598-602). Indeed, Donne did not hesitate to uphold the view of Cartwright that if preaching stopped, the Church itself would fail: "So how long soever Christ have dwelt in any State, or any Church, if he grow speechless, he is departing, if there be a discontinuing, or slackning of preaching, there is a danger of loosing Christ" (VII, 5, 692-95).[27]

On almost every issue raised in the debate between Whitgift and Cartwright concerning what the sermon was and what it was intended to accomplish, Donne sided with the Puritan wing against the orthodox conservative thinking of the Church. He was totally in accord with Cartwright's contention that "the *ordinary* and especial means to work faith is by preaching and not reading . . . It is the excellentest and most *ordinary* means to work faith by in the hearts of the hearers . . . The *ordinary* ways whereby God regenerateth his children is by the Word of God which is preached."[28]

Remarkable as this insight into Donne's theoretical conception of the sermon is, its literary significance depends upon the practice, and this requires that we explore more closely the relationship of the preacher to preaching.

We have already shown that Donne saw preaching as an encounter with Christ mediated through the personality of the preacher. This, of course, introduces a subjective uncertainty into the event which can be contrasted to the objectively concrete nature of the Eucharist. It might be plausibly argued that if preaching operates on an *ex opere* basis, the preached Word being in fact the Word of God, then we should expect the personality of the preacher to be submerged so that only the voice of Christ be heard. If this is true, how do we account for the paradox created by Donne's celebrated "personality" which virtually all readers acknowledge to run through his sermons? We are reminded of T. S. Eliot's opinion that Donne "is dangerous . . . for those who, fascinated by 'personality' in the romantic sense of the word — for those who find in 'personality' an ultimate value — forget that in

27. Thomas Cartwright, quoted in Hooker, *Laws,* V, xxi, 4.
28. *Ibid.,* V, xxi, 3.

the spiritual hierarchy there are places higher than that of Donne."[29]

Actually, the paradox is only apparent, not real. It rests upon a misconception of the nature of the preacher's instrumentality. God chose man as his medium, Donne felt, because it was the only possible means of communication. "Nothing can speak, but man" he insisted, "No voice is understood by man, but the voice of man . . . The same voice from heaven, the same word of God, but speaking in the ministry of man" (VI, 6, 487-95). God, it would seem, intentionally spoke to imperfect men through imperfect means. In no other way was dialogue possible. Ernest Best aptly characterizes the situation when he says, "God has chosen these weak vessels, preachers, that by them he may meet men, just as he chose weak men as the writers of Scripture. We recognize that through the personalities of the latter we encounter God as we read their writings; part of the fundamentalist heresy lies in its practical denial of the personality of the biblical writers. To import the same demand for 'anonymity' into preaching is to seek a similar infallibility which God by his very choise of men has ruled out."[30] The *ex opere* principle, we may conclude, does not demand a preacher's "anonymity" at all. To the contrary, in preaching, the Word of God and the words of men meet in sacred synthesis. This, perhaps, can be expressed more precisely through a christological analogy: just as the divine and human natures "are related in the one Person, so are the divine and human words in the one sermon."[31] Of course, in the sermon it is not two perfections that are joined but divine perfection and human imperfection, so that Donne, reflecting Calvin's caution,[32] conceded that "all the sermon is not Gods word, but all the Sermon is Gods Ordinance, and the Text is certainely his word" (VII, 12, 720-21).

The practical application of this theory brings us closer to

---

29. T. S. Eliot, "Lancelot Andrewes," *Essays Ancient and Modern* (New York, 1932), pp. 22-23.

30. Ernest Best, "Two Modes of Encounter: An Exposition of the Relationship of the Eucharist and Preaching," *Interpretation,* XVII (1963), 29.

31. Best, 29.

32. See Ronald S. Wallace, *Calvin's Doctrine of the Word and Sacrament* (Grand Rapids, Mich., 1957), pp. 89-90.

an explanation of Donne's intrusion of "personality" into his sermons. If the preacher realizes his function as an instrument through which the Word of God is mediated, he must, at the same time, be aware of his responsibility to make himself as efficient an instrument as possible. He does this not only through diligent study and dedication to Creed and doctrine, but also through attention to subjective urgings which he must assume to be the promptings of the Holy Spirit: "God directs the tongue of his Ministers, as he doth showres of rain," Donne preached. "They fall upon the face of a large compasse of earth, when as all that earth did not need that rain" (VII, 13, 110-12). Moreover, the matter and format of the sermon were determined by Holy promptings: "And yet God directs us sometimes to extend our discourse (perhaps with a zeale and a vehemence, which may seem unnecessary and impertinent, because all the Church are presumed to be of one mind) in the proofe of our doctrine against Papists" (VII, 13, 114-18). In short, Donne understood his subjective feelings to be divinely inspired in his preaching and, in this regard, his fondness for the preaching of David becomes obvious. "He [David] goes not far for his Example," Donne observed, "He labors not to shew his reading, but his feeling; not his learning, but his compunction; his Conscience is his Library, and his Example is himselfe, and he does not unclaspe great Volumes, but unbutton his owne breast, and from thence takes it" (IX, 12, 137-41).

The danger inherent in such confidence in subjective feelings is, of course, that it incurs the problem of ascertaining which impulses are divine and which are human. Certainly a preacher could test the authencity of his feelings against the written Scriptures and Church dogma, but a total reliance on this recourse would represent a betrayal of the *ex opere* doctrine and the dynamic comprehension of the preached Word that it presupposed. The preacher's main warrant, therefore, had to lie in a confidence that preaching was an ordinance of God and that the duly-ordained minister in the act of preaching was a divine instrument who "can claim no more at Gods hand, for this service [preaching], then the Sun can, for shining upon the earth, or the earth for producing flowers, and fruits" (X, 5, 265-67).

We can see that the homiletic convictions of John Donne which distinguish him from his Anglo-Catholic brethren (the dynamic conception of the Word of God, the application of the *ex opere* principle to preaching, and the sacramental estimation of the sermon event) served to give his sermons a peculiar functional distinction. They were geared to produce crisis, to change men's lives by bringing them into direct confrontation with their God. Donne's intention was not merely to edify the intellect; it was primarily to strike the conscience. "It is not the depth, nor the wit, nor the eloquence of the Preacher that pierces us," he counseled, "but his neareness; that he speaks to my conscience." (III, 5, 295-97). This is but another way of expressing E. Winston Jones' observation that "though generally so regarded, the sermon is not directed to the mind alone, but to the entire psycho-physical organism, which is much more than the mind."[33]

Without a doubt, a communiqué to the conscience must employ radically different means from a communiqué to the mind, with or without the assistance of the Holy Ghost. If it is true that "a person changed against his will is of the same opinion still,[34] we can see that logic and argument have only a temporary effect, if any, and that a "permanent change can be accomplished only by shifting the base of fundamental point of attachment."[35] The problem for Donne was to preach to this fundamental point of attachment, to touch the conscience of his congregation, and this required special technique.

Donne's solution was remarkably simple. He preached "himselfe." "When a preacher preaches himselfe," he confided, "and his own sense of Gods mercies, or Judgments upon him, as that is intended most for the glory of God, so it should be applied most by the hearer, for his own edification" (IX, 12, 207-10). This preaching of one's self might at first glance seem to be an effective pastoral technique only if the preacher was assumed to be a model for his congregation to emulate. Such an assumption ignores the *ex opere* principle behind the technique. Aside from the quite unChristian presumption inherent in such a rationale, it is clear that a seventeenth-century Anglican would hardly have found the

33. *Preaching and the Dramatic Arts* (New York, 1948), p. 2.
34. *Ibid.,* p. 4.
35. Robert T. Oliver, *The Psychology of Persuasive Speech* (London, 1942), p. 257.

most commodious route to Christ by following in the footsteps of the then Dean of St. Paul's. The layman was not expected to imitate his pastor; he was expected to imitate Christ. By preaching himself, Donne was merely assuming that his faith and ordination assured the divine instrumentality of his very imperfections. What the man in the pew experienced was an extraordinary conspiracy of minister and Holy Ghost working to bring about an awareness of his salvation.

One reason why the current vogue of existentialist interpretation has been applied to Donne's sermons[36] is probably that the type of communication employed in them is so apparently congenial to the existentialist's problem of transferring subjective truth from one individual to another. Søren Kierkegaard, for example, remarked in his *Concluding Unscientific Postscript* that "Existential reality is incommunicable, and the subjective thinker finds his reality in his own ethical existence. When reality is apprehended by an outsider it can be understood only as possibility. Everyone who makes a communication, insofar as he becomes conscious of this fact, will therefore be careful to give his existential communication the form of possibility, precisely in order that he may have a relationship to existence."[37]

As secular explanation of sacramental experience, Kierkegaard's statement has relevance to Donne's sermons. Donne would have agreed that reality is to be found in "ethical existence" (conscience), and he would have also agreed that there was a problem in transferring that reality from one subjective entity to another. What is lacking in Kierkegaard's account is the divine participation which gives the sermon its unique distinction. It is the Holy Ghost present in the sermon event which makes possible the "possibility" that Kierkegaard speaks of. Ministers in the pulpit were not, in Donne's view, mere men, urgently mouthing possibilities to other men; "The Ministers of God are Sonnes of Thunder, They are falls of water, trampling of horses, and runnings of Chariots" (V, 16, 134-35). Preachers were apocalyptic messengers, animated

36. See, for example, William R. Mueller, *John Donne: Preacher* (Princeton, 1962), p. 241.

37. *Concluding Unscientific Postscript,* trans. David F. Swenson and Walter Lowrie (Princeton, 1941), p. 169.

by the Holy Spirit, who brought God into dynamic encounter with Christians. "We should preach his glory, his power," said Donne, "that every man might speake one anothers language, and preach to one anothers conscience; that when I accuse my selfe, and confesse mine infirmities to another man, that man may understand, that there is, in that confession of mine, a Sermon" (V, 1, 754-57).

The *ex opere* doctrine provided the glue which bound together the Word of God and Donne's glorious preaching of himself. Through its warrant, Donne satisfied himself that the preacher "hides none of his owne sins; none of those practices, which he had formerly used to hide his sins: He confesses things there, which none know but himselfe . . . and poures out his own soule to the Congregation, in letting them know, how long the Lord let him run on in vanities, and vexation of spirit, and how powerfully and effectually he reclaimed him at last" (IX, 12, 184-96).

The fruits of Donne's homiletic convictions have elicited the famous criticism of T. S. Eliot that Donne "is a little of the religious spellbinder, the Reverend Billy Sunday of his time, the flesh-creeper, the sorcerer of emotional orgy."[38] While we may object to the lurid diction of this appraisal, there is considerable truth to what Eliot says. More significant, however, is the context out of which this opinion emerges. It is the Anglo-Catholic Bishop Andrewes to whom he is comparing Donne, and it is not difficult to hear in Eliot's almost perverse perference of Andrewes over Donne the echo of Richard Hooker's indignation at Thomas Cartwright. Eliot is very much the conservative, exhibiting, it would seem, a bit of *ex post facto* alarm over the excessive enthusiasm he finds in Donne's sermons. Donne, he says, lacks a proper *"goût pour la vie spirituelle"*[39] because "there is always the something else, the 'baffling' " in his preaching. Most of all, it is the fact that Donne is a " 'personality' in a sense which Andrewes is not " that bothers Eliot.

Eliot, obviously, is Hooker, the homiletician, re-incarnated, undoubtedly sharing his view that the sermon should assault the

38. Eliot, pp. 9-10.
39. *Ibid.*, p. 21.

intellect, not the conscience, that the Word of God is statically imprinted on paper, not dynamically presented in preaching. On what other bases could he praise Andrewes' preaching on grounds that "reading Andrewes . . . is like listening to a great Hellenist expounding a text of the *Posterior Analytics*"[40].

Clearly there is a vast chasm separating the preaching of Andrewes and Donne, but it is a chasm not so much of personality and rhetoric as dogma. Basic as the Word of God is to the Christian community, it is no less basic to the distinctive styles of its messengers. "In the beginning was the Word," begins the Gospel according to St. John, "and the Word was with God, and the Word was God." In the profoundest sense this was the homiletic gospel of another John — John Donne. No other statement serves as well to sum up his preaching theory than this.

40. *Ibid.*, pp. 13-4.

Chapter Ten
Performative Preaching

The sacramental quality of the sermon, which the last chapter sought to emphasize, should impress us with the fact that preaching (at least as it was viewed by those of Donne's persuasion) is not primarily a rhetorical but a kerygmatic act. Sermons ought not to be something we analyze, but events through which we understand. To put it another way, the sacramental sermon *contains* the reality it describes; the Word of God within it is not a language in detachment from God but the very coming of God Himself. Like music and poetry, the sermon *is* in its expression, and we should be very careful in selecting a system of interrogation of preaching texts that we do justice to the uniqueness of this kind of language.

Just as with poetic devotions, I feel that the most appropriate and rewarding interrogation of sermon literature springs directly from its religious intention — questions which reflect a utilitarian rather than an aesthetic bias. Understandably, I enthusiastically applaud Joan Webber's statement that "Donne is leading his congregation through a meditation, and the process of thought involved in meditation has really as much to do with the style of his sermons as do any conclusions from which they begin and to which they return again."[1] The meditative "process of thought" and subsequent style which characterize Donne's sermons fit a category of language that I call performative God-talk, for they comprise a system of utterances committed to *doing* rather than *saying*.

I ought to admit from the start that much of what I shall put forward as an alternative to a *literary* criticism of sermons is frankly speculative and in no way conceived as a rival to the superb rhetorical studies by Joan Webber nor the valuable contributions on Donne's sermons by Dennis Quinn and, most recently,

---

1. *Contrary Music: The Prose Style of John Donne* (Madison: University of Wisconsin Press, 1963), p. 43.

Winfried Schleiner. My intent is merely to suggest that additional *literary* insight into the sermons might be gained by deliberately assuming a non-literary perspective, a perspective, that is, which subordinates all concerns to the overriding one of religious utility.

I should also try to lay to rest any anxiety that I may be recklessly considering all the elements of the sermon to be the Word of God or even pure God-talk. Donne, we recall, cautioned that "all the sermon is not Gods word," even while he was insisting that "all the Sermon is Gods Ordinance" (VII, 12, 720-21), and I take this to mean that he wished to make a distinction between the dynamic proclamation of the redemptive event (kerygma) and the subsequent teaching based upon it (didache).[2] The sermon, in other words, is a mixed bag, blending didactic and revelatory elements in patterns that are not often predictable. For this reason, I make no claim that performative God-talk pervades the sermons in any absolute sense. I will claim, however, that it determines the sermon's semantic structure — its language-game — so that even the didactic elements are ultimately pressed into its service.

We are familiar enough with the general nature of God-talk to recognize its activity in a given text, and I would like to begin by examining a specific sermon preached by Donne for its God-talk content. I have chosen the sermon randomly from the Potter, Simpson collection. It is based on Isaiah 7:14 ("Therefore the Lord Shall Give You A Signe; Behold, A Virgin Shall Conceive, and Beare A Son, and Shall Call His Name Immanuel") and was preached at St. Paul's on Christmas Evening, 1624.

Even as Donne "divides" his text in this sermon he appears to be injecting from the start a substantial dosage of logical impropriety. He begins with a model from grammar: the conjunction. He recalls how St. Bernard "spent his consideration upon three remarkable conjunctions, this day. First, a Conjunction of God, and Man in one person, Christ Jesus; Then a conjunction of the

2. I am employing C. H. Dodd's distinctions here, which I take to contrast the dynamic proclamation of the redemptive event (*kerygma*) with static systems of doctrine (*didache*). See *The Apostolic Preaching and Its Developments* (London: Hodder & Stoughton, 1936), p. 6. Further treatment on the distinction between *kerygma* and *didache* can be found in Edmund P. Clowney, *Preaching and Biblical Theology* (London: Tyndale Press, 1962), p. 23.

incompatible Titles, Maid and Mother, in one blessed woman, the blessed Virgin *Mary*; And thirdly a conjunction of Faith, and the Reason of man, that so beleeves, and comprehends those two conjunctions" (VI, 8, 1-6). St. Bernard succinctly joins the major miraculous paradoxes of Christianity (the Incarnation, the Immaculate Conception) in series with what takes on the miraculous through association, the presumably paradoxical yoking of faith and reason in man. To this trinity of paradoxical miracles, strange as they are in themselves, Donne adds a fourth "strange conjunction": "*Propterea, Therefore*: for that joynes the anger of God, and his mercy together" (VI, 8, 7-9).

What Donne was after all along was a context in which Isaiah 7:14 might be seen in a paradoxical rather than an inferential light. He wanted to stress its *non*-rational rather than its rational logic, and so the focal point of the text becomes the conjunction "Therefore." Grammatically, "Therefore" is an illative. It formally introduces the conclusion to a line of deduction. And yet to make sure that the logical *im*propriety of the deduction that Isaiah has evoked in Donne's mind is also evoked in the minds of his congregation, he introduces it with a series of traditional Christian logical improprieties: the Incarnation, the Virgin Birth, the paradox of reason and faith. Here is a case of a grammatical model, "Therefore," finding religious qualification through the preparatory laying of an odd context. Donne has his prize: the paradoxicality of God's anger precipitating a show of his mercy. He has exploited the superficial grammatical logic which "Therefore" apparently heralds in order to bring into bold relief the paradoxically *il*-logical (from the "reasonable" and grammatical point of view) behavior of God.

From the beginning of this sermon Donne has caused battle lines to form between two disparate logical planes. On the one side he places the logic of reason with its peculiar set of motives, causes and expectations all culminating in the key illative, "Therefore." On the other side, he presses the logic of faith which works through its different set of motives, causes and expectations toward the same binding "Therefore." "Therefore" thus marks the tangency of two rival language-games, and with predictable adroitness Donne leads his auditory out of one and into the other: "God chides and rebukes the King *Achaz* by the Prophet, he is angry with him, and *Therefore*, sayes the Text, because he is angry he will give him a signe, a seale of mercy" (VI, 8, 9-11). Hence Donne introduces his first "generall consideration, that Gods mercy is alwaies in season" (VI, 8, 19-20).

To evoke an understanding of God's infinite mercy, Donne must somehow effect a leap from man's sense of mercy to an intuition of the qualitatively distinct divine mercy. The characteristic way with which God-talk deals with such problems is to provide a series of self-denying images and assertions in the hope that an accumulation of these will somehow complement one another and precipitate an appropriately religious discernment of the reality, say, of God's mercy. This is exactly Donne's procedure. He begins his discussion of mercy on the models of first sequence and then time. Both sequence and time, of course, belong to the context of Reason rather than Faith. "As God made grasse for beasts, before he made beasts, and beasts, before he made beasts, and beasts for man: As in that first generation, the Creation, so in the regeneration, our re-creating, he begins with that which was necessary for that which followes, Mercy before Judgement" (VI, 8, 64-68). Here is Donne employing a highly rational analogue involving sequence and time to get at a divine virtue whose infiniteness is an explicit *denial* of the categories of sequence and time. The analogy is highly inadequate, and Donne knows it. He further knows that *any* analogy he uses, no matter how superficially comprehensive and fitting it might appear, is of necessity going to be inadequate also. His method — the method of God-talk — is to throw as many images, analogies and assertions, with all their contradictions, paradoxes and irrationalities, together — to let them "correct" one another's excessive anthropomorphism, to restrict one another's monopolistic and inherently idolatrous intents.

In this first rational analogy based on time and sequence, Donne has managed to establish a priority between God's mercy and judgment. Mercy comes first, of course, but in making that point, he has been forced to push mercy into an inappropriate temporal category. He must now "correct" his first analogy. "Nay," he says, "to say that mercy was first, is but to post-date mercy; to preferre mercy but so, is to diminish mercy: The names of first or last derogate from it, for first and last are but ragges of time, and his mercy hath no relation to time, it is not first, nor

last, but eternall, everlasting" (VI, 8, 68-73). The model of time, useful for establishing the priority of mercy over judgment, is itself
denied once its usefulness is past, and even the experience of the
denial is turned to further exhortatory service: "Let the Devill
make me so far desperate as to conceive a time when there was no
mercy, and he hath made me so far an Atheist, as to conceive a
time when there was no God; if I despoile him of his mercy, any
one minute, and say, now God hath no mercy, for that minute I
discontinue his very God-head, and his beeing" (VI, 8, 73-77).
How perilously close Donne himself came to committing the sin
he describes here in his first analogy of time! Without the qualifying self-denial of the analogy, the road to Atheism Donne spells
out would be clearly before us.

Donne's characteristic existential point of view toward
divine knowledge[3] shows itself as well in this passage on mercy,
particularly in his own description of the very hermeneutical task
he is at that moment performing. "So then," he preaches, "here
we consider not mercy as it is radically in God, an essential attribute of his, but productively in us, as it is an action, a working
upon us" (VI, 8, 86-88). This passage also serves as a transition
from a discussion of the "generall consideration" of mercy to an
opening of the issue of "particular mercies." A variety of images
are raised to characterize God's particular mercies to individuals:
mercies are "feathers of his wings . . . that cloud of Quailes, which
hovered over the host of Israel," and the prayers petitioning these
mercies are "our birdlime . . . our net to catch, our Gomer to fill
those Quailes" (VI, 8, 90-94). To complement the natural bird
images with theit obvious restrictive limitations upon the scope of
divine mercy, Donne juxtaposes a scientific image of plenitude
which literally contradicts but figuratively amplifies the birds of
mercy: "The aire is not so full of Moats, of Atomes, as the Church
is of Mercies: and we can suck in no part of aire, but we take in
those Moats, those Atomes" (VI, 8, 94-96). To bring the point
existentially home to his listeners, he adds, ". . . so here in the

---

3. The point of Donne's "existential" posture toward preaching has been
made by Theodore Gill in his Introduction to *The Sermons of John Donne*
(New York: Meridian, 1958), and by William R. Mueller, *John Donne:
Preacher* (Princeton: Princeton University Press, 1962), p. 241.

Congregation we cannot suck in a word from the preacher, we cannot speak, we cannot sigh a prayer to God, but that the whole breath and aire is made of mercy" (VI, 8, 97-99).

In attempting to evoke the quality of God's mercy Donne uses an extremely wide variety of images, each one working independently on a single facet of an ineffable whole, unabashedly contradicting its fellow images, and yet simultaneously throwing additional light upon them as well. Because he understands the nature of God-talk, Donne feels no qualms about speaking of mercy at one point essentially (as material substance), at another linguistically (as word), at still another existentially (as act). If he were merely seeking to produce a consistent, logical mapping of God's mercy for his congregation, this kind of procedure would have been indefensible. But Donne was not *defining* mercy; he was trying to effect a disclosure of it, and his homiletic problem was: How do I evoke the *distinctive* and *unique* disclosure of divine mercy by means of a language largely regimented by custom and tradition?

The answer, of course, is implicit in the Scriptures themselves. Ian Ramsey tells us that the earliest evangelists met the identical problem Donne faced in "a rough and ready way by taking as many traditional phrases as they could, and mixing them in the most riotous manner possible."[4] This was an attempt, Ramsey goes on to explain, "to secure that special logical impropriety needed to express the Christian message. Each word is logically qualified by the presence of the others, and in this way each word comes to display a suitable measure of impropriety." As with the early evangelists, Donne was after "logical impropriety" too, not so that he could more effectively *inform* his auditory, but so that he could create "self-involving"[5] situations in which each man in the pew was confronted by a personal self-disclosure.

Metaphorical inconsistency, then, is an unavoidable feature of any form of God-talk, no less preached God-talk, and Donne's

4. *Religious Language: An Empirical Placing of Theological Phrases* (New York: MacMillan, 1957), p. 178.

5. The term is Donald D. Evans', *The Logic of Self-Involvement* (London: SCM Press, 1963), pp. 125-35, 249-52. Reprinted in *Words About God*, ed. Ian T. Ramsey (London: SCM Press, 1971), pp. 224-36.

use of contradictory figures of speech is not a measure of his carelessness, originality, nor undisciplined imagination, but a reflection of his linguistic commitment to his ordination. Donne's ministerial duty demanded his acknowledgment that an orderly faith more often than not required a deliberately "disorderly" language.

But even beyond the matter of metaphor Donne's pulpit God-talk is governed by an underlying logical premise which sets it apart from secular orations. That "underlying logical premise" might best be explained in terms of what Donald Evans calls "onlook attitudes."[6] The coinage "onlook" derives from the linguistic formula most people resort to when they form an opinion: "I look on death as the mockery of human hopes," for example, or "I look on sex as a sordid animal urge." After examining many "onlook" statements, Evans discovers that their nature is essentially "Commissive and Verdictive." He points out that "in saying, 'I look on x as y', I commit myself to a policy of behaviour and thought and I register my decision that x is appropriately described as y; my utterance combines an undertaking with a judgment. One cannot abstract what is undertaken (for example, in relation to my suffering) from my view of it (for example, as God's discipline)."[7] In may ways, onlook assertions are comparable to the discernment-commitment situations which Ramsey contends are at the heart of all religious language. At any rate, there is a world of difference between a statement of fact and a statement of onlook; whereas the former is authoritatively subject to demonstrable evidence, the latter is subject to an attitude and is hence "self-involving." As Evans succinctly summarizes, "The expression of an onlook commits me to a way of behaving and thinking, a mode of life."[8]

I am convinced that sermons are not properly understood unless they are considered as being made up of related onlook assertions. Indeed, the Sermon by definition is contextually dominated by a distinct religious onlook (the acknowledgment of the existence of God) which makes it impossible for it to include,

6. *Words About God,* pp. 225 ff.
7. *Ibid.,* pp. 227-28.
8. *Ibid.,* p. 235.

in Evans' words, "an event or entity which can be (or could have been) reported *neutrally* — regardless of one's onlooks or other attitudes."[9] Sermon language, then, is necessarily *attitudinal* language committed to an acknowledged onlook, so that when Donne makes such remarks as "God calls not upon us, to be considered as God in himself, but as God towards us" (I, 4, 427-28), he is merely re-affirming the established controlling onlook which governs the very semantic substructure of any genuine sermon-event. Donne "looks on" God, in other words, not in Himself but within an attitudinal context — not ontologically but, if you will, existentially. He assumes that his auditory will subsume all of his assertions to the overriding logic of that onlook.

There are, of course, onlooks which are inappropriate to God-talk and therefore to the sermon as well, onlooks which are analogous to what I have elsewhere called "stand-in" metaphors. These are onlooks which are didactic rather than revelatory in nature. Evans, as a matter of fact, calls them "analogical" as opposed to "parabolic" onlooks and supplies a list of contrasting examples to illustrate the distinction:

    (I)   'I look on Henry as a brother.'
             'I look on Smith as a tool.'
             'I look on the vicar as my shepherd.'
    (II)   'I look on music as a language.'
             'I look on alcoholism as a disease.'
             'I look on Adenauer as the architect of the new Germany.'[10]

In the first set of examples "the similarity which is implied between *x* and *y* is mainly in terms of appropriate attitude: *x* is *such that* the attitude appropriate to *y* is similar to the attitude appropriate to *x*." Onlooks such as these Evans identifies as parabolic. In the second list, however, a similarity is suggested "which is independent of any similarity of appropriate attitude. The meaning of 'I look on *x* as *y*' can here be readily analyzed by abstracting a content (for example, 'alcoholism is a disease') and then adding autobiographical and commissive elements." Onlooks such as these are analogical. To summarize, in an analogical onlook there is a more-or-less neutral core of content residing accessible

9. *Ibid.*
10. *Ibid.,* p. 231.

within an attitudinal context. In a parabolic onlook, however, no such core is extractable except in parabolic form.

My contention is that the natural structure of sermon logic is inevitably related to the conduct of parabolic onlooks if for no other reason than that its overriding point of view is itself a parabolic onlook: "I look on God as . . ." As Evans points out, "It is not a matter of acting as if I believed that God is like a father. Rather, I actually do believe that God is like a father; but what I mean by this is to be explained in terms of human attitudes: I believe that God is *such that* the attitude appropriate to Him is similar to that which is appropriate towards a human father."[11] Sermons are connected parabolic onlooks because their functional thrust is determinedly self-involving, commissive and verdictive.

Returning to Donne's Christmas sermon, we might find it helpful to look at Donne's various treatments of specific Christian dogma as parabolic onlooks rather than conventionally-conceived analogies. I think we will discover in the process how the structure of the sermon necessarily varies from the structure of the disquisition. In a sense, of course, I have already made implicit use of the concept of parabolic onlooks in discussing Donne's treatment of divine mercy. The apparently inconsistent and contradictory metaphors that Donne used to evoke a sense of divine mercy find instant reconciliation as soon as they are considered within the framework of: "I look on God's mercy as . . .". Since attitude rather than essence is the goal in a parabolic onlook, almost any metaphor is legitimate as long as it promotes the ultimate attitudinal insight. An existential end, if you will, justifies inconsistent essential means.

11. *Ibid.*, p. 232. Evans cites the following corroboration from Edwyn Bevan (*Symbolism and Belief* [London, 1938], pp. 335-6): "The Theist or Christian does not merely say: 'Act as if there were a God who is a loving Father, and you will find certain desirable results follow' (that is Pragmatism): he says, 'Act as if there were a God who is a loving Father, and you will, in so doing, be making the right response to that which God really is. God is really of such a character that, if any of us could know Him as He is (which we cannot do) and then had to describe in human language to men upon earth what we saw, he would have to say: 'What I see is undescribable, but if you think of God as a loving Father, I cannot put the reality to you in a better way than that: that is the nearest you can get.' "

When Donne confronts the Incarnation in this sermon, he seems not to be embarrassed at all by its mystery. As a matter of fact, he seems to go out of his way to point out its inaccessibility to human reason. After ticking off the various scholastic explanations of the meaning of God-made-flesh by Hilary, Damascen and Irenaeus, all at best analogical onlooks, Donne finally falls back to embrace "*S. Basils* modesty, and abstinence, *Nativitas ista silentio honoretur,* This mysterie is not so well celebrated, with our words, and discourse, as with a holy silence, and meditation" (VI, 8, 402-404). His intent in peremptorily dismissing the patristic rationalizations of the Incarnation in favor of St. Basil's silence is largely, I think, to clear the way for a quite different approach, a self-involving one. He wants to avoid any objective, neutral dealing with the mystery in order that its human reference be placed in sharp focus. He even prepares for this by methodically emphasizing the non-human, non-temporal nature of the Nativity. The prophecy of Christ's birth delivered to Achaz six hundred years before the event itself is, as Donne insistently underscores, a matter beyond our temporal categoes: "Now, how is this future thing, (There shall be a Messias) a signe of their present deliverance from that siege? First, In the notion of the Prophet, it was not a future thing; for, as in Gods owne sight, so in their sight, to whom he opens himselfe, future things are present" (VI, 8, 357-61). Furthermore, we are not to be "over-vehement, over-peremptory, (so far, as to the perplexing of thine owne reason and understanding, or so far, as to the despising of the reasons of other men) in calculating the time, the day or houre of this nativity" (VI, 8, 409-12). Still further: we should "never come to that question, how it was done" (VI, 8, 415). True, Donne is in one sense discouraging an unbecoming intellectual hybris in the face of divine mystery, but he is also rejecting an insiginificant and unrewarding rational approach to the Incarnation in favor of a religiously salutary faith onlook, an onlook which parabolically "explains" the Incarnation in terms of *human* values. This is the only acceptable onlook for a sermon-event, and it is clear that Donne has organized his assertions about the simple onlook formula: I look on the Incarnation as "a signe to mee, that God, and I, shall never bee parted" (VI, 8, 421-22). This resolution is far from what we could describe as an inferential one: to the contrary, the true nature of the resolution is "self-involving."

Almost the entire remainder of this sermon is devoted to a "signe" of the "signe in generall," the Virgin Birth, and at first glance, it might appear that Donne himself is engaging in the kind of "contentious wrangling" of which he so often accuses the scholastic theologians. He seems to plunge into the thick of the controversy, exhuming heresies here, challenging ambiguities there, in ways that appear unrewarding to the sacramental aim of the sermon-event. The appearance, however, is not the reality, a fact which becomes quite clear as soon as we understand Donne's "contentious wrangling" as a consistent, ongoing process toward the development of a self-involving parabolic look. What Donne is desperately interested to accomplish here is a manipulation of attitude in his congregation. He wants his auditory to confront the mysteries of the faith not as insoluble problems of biology, physics, deduction or metaphysics, for these would be unrewarding "neutral" approaches to Christian doctrine which have no proper place within the sacramental context of the sermon. Donne, as preacher, does not wish to *prove a point* in the fashion of those patristic authorities to whom he alludes; he wants instead to clear away all such rational, neutral considerations of Christian mysteries in order to wrap them in the more appropriate language of self-involvement. How does he do this?

He does it, I am convinced, by a careful screening of onlooks. He wants to sweep aside all *analogical* onlooks, which would permit the Virgin Birth to be considered independently of human attitude, in order to get at that mystery's function as sign. His procedure is to bring forward a variety of positions on the subject all the way from Pliny to Calvin, dismissing all those which make no reference to human attitude — all those, in other words, which are not self-involving. The position toward the Virgin Birth most fatal to its potential self-involving capability is obviously the one which denies its uniqueness — the one which tries to assimilate the Virgin Birth into the natural order. Donne begins his housekeeping here by brushing aside the claims of Gellius and Pliny "that a Virgin had a child, almost 200. yeares before Christ," along with the report by Genebrard "that the like fell out in France", in his time. These authorities, Donne comments, "are not within our faith, and they are without our reason; our faith stoopes not downe to them, and our reason reaches not up to them" (VI, 8, 429-33). In rejecting these men, Donne provisionally defines the proper bounds of Christian inquiry, an area in which speculative reasoning is appropriately held on Faith's leash. Perhaps more telling, however, is his pursuit of essentially the same point with reference to Aquinas' citation "that in the times of *Constantine* and *Irene*, upon a dead body found in a sepulchre, there was found this inscription, in a plate of gold, *Christus nacetur ex Virgine, & ego credo in eum*, Christ shall be borne of a Virgin, and I beleeve in that Christ" (VI, 8, 434-38). Here is a piece of empirically-verified prophecy which, to the religiously unsophisticated eye, might seem, at first, a boon. And yet Donne is very nervous about it. "If this be true," he remarks, "yet our ground is not upon such testimonie; If God had not said it, I would never have beleeved it" (VI, 8, 441-43).

Donne is, of course, concerned about the *source* of belief here. To believe on the basis of empirical evidence is hardly a self-involved belief. It reflects an onlook which is straightforward, requiring no real reference to human attitude. The onlook formula for this case would actually read like this: I look on the Virgin Birth as an *a posteriori* confirmation of an event predicted in history. The onlook bypasses any self-involving reference to an attitude (in this case faith), and this is why Donne carefully qualifies his position toward the significance of the piece of evidence. He does not believe because of the testimony on the gold plate; he believes on the basis of God's Word: "If God had not said it, I would never have beleeved it .... That this Mother, in our text, was a Virgin, is a peculiar, a singular sign, given, as such, by God; never done but then" (VI, 8, 442-50). Donne's onlook formula, therefore, reads like this: I look on the Virgin Birth as a sign. There is nothing neutral about such an onlook, for the factuality of the phenomenon is ruled not the issue. The entire burden of the Virgin Birth is its function as a sign of God's attitude toward man, and man's attitude toward God.

Donne dutifully turns to a consideration of three heresies on the Virgin Birth which "impeach the virginity of this most blessed Woman: The Corinthians said she conceived by ordinary generation; *Iovinian* said, she was delivered by ordinary meanes; And *Helvidius* said, she had children after" (VI, 8, 483). Obviously, Donne wants to preserve the miraculous mystery of the Immaculate Conception against all attempts to accommodate it to the natural order and the natural understanding. His dealing with the heresies is understandably orthodox and routine because here is a case where dogma is precisely consonant with the sacramental intention of his preaching. Here the Church itself acknowledges in its ruling that self-involving exegesis is to be consistently preferred to "neutral" exegesis, and Donne, of course, has no quarrel.

Some of the rigor with which Donne scrutinizes the issue of the Virgin Birth for *non*-self-involving elements is visible in his delicate scolding of Luther, who he feels becomes tempted by the authority of sheer logic to forego momentarily his obligation to the authority of faith. *"Luther* was awake, and risen, but he was not readie," says Donne. "Hee had seene light, and looked toward it, but yet saw not so clearly by it, then, when he said, That the blessed Virgin was of a middle condition, betweene Christ, and man; that man hath his conception, and his quickning (by the infusion of the soule) in originall sin; that Christ had it in neither, no sin in his conception, none in his animation, in the infusion of his soule" (VI, 8, 542-49). Up to this point the substantive quarrel between Donne and Luther would seem to be over the status of the blessed Virgin: is she superhuman, that is, in a state above man but below Christ? Donne insists that she is not, but more significant that the apparent remonstance against Mariolatry in his scolding of Luther is his nervousness over the quality of what we might call Luther's onlook on the matter. This is clear from Donne's following statement: "But, saies Luther, howsoever it were at the conception, certainly at the inanimation, at the quickning, she was preserved from originall sin" (VI, 8, 549-51). To this, Donne retorts, "Now, what needs this? may I not say, that I had rather be redeemed by Christ Jesus then bee innocent? rather be beholden to Christs death, for my salvation, then to *Adams* standing in his innocencie? " (VI, 8, 554). Donne's point, and the burden of his complaint against Luther, is that Luther is permitting a neutral logical deduction (that because Christ should not be understood to have been conceived nor animated in original sin, therefore, Mary's status must be exalted to avoid such an eventuality) to compromise the self-involving significance of the Virgin Birth as sign. The conundrum Donne seems to pose is purely rhetorical: Which is more important to the Christian, to be re-deemed or to be innocent? Innocence, of course, lacks the self-involving attitude of commitment that redemption implies; the former is more-or-less verifiable, while the latter involves a commitment of attitude.

The final division of Donne's text isolates the significance of Christ's name, *"Immanuel, God with us"* (VI, 8, 615), and Donne uses this occasion to provide further clarification on his quarrel with Luther. Donne makes a point of emphasizing that "she [Mary], and shee onely knew that he [Christ] was the Sonne of God, and not of naturall generation by man" (VI, 8, 575-77). Mary's unique "knowledge," Donne is eager to establish, is tanta-mount to the regenerate sinner's faith, for near the conclusion to the sermon he defines the regenerate sinner (the "worthy hearer") as he who "can call this Lord, this Jesus, this Christ, *Immanuel, God with us*" (VI, 8, 614-15). The capability of honestly calling Jesus, Immanuel, God with us, Donne sets up as an absolute test of faith and then further elucidates the applicability of this test to Mary's virginal purity by clearly stating: ". . . onely that Virgin soule, devirginated in the blood of *Adam,* but restored in the blood of the Lambe, hath this *Ecce,* this testimony, this assurance, that God is with him" (VI, 8, 615-17). Very delicately, Donne is pressing the point that "virginity" is appropriately a status of *attitude,* faith, if you will, whatever biological status it may also denote. The technical question of Mary's physical virginity is, to Donne's mind, somehow beside the point. Mary's "knowledge" (faith) assures her purity as Christ's mother; that she can call her baby *"Immanuel, Christ with us"* is proof that her "Virgin soule, devirginated in the blood of *Adam"* has truly been "restored in the blood of the Lambe." With this in mind, it is not difficult to understand Donne's pique at Luther. Donne sees the whole issue of Virgin Birth within a language-game governed by the logic of faith. He is disappointed in Luther for having been lured out of what Donne feels is the appropriate language-game for discussing the question. Luther, he feels, makes an altogether "unnecessary" and religiously damaging concession to biological fact. "Now, what needs this? " Donne understandably replies to Luther's notion that Mary was of a "middle condition." Luther dropped a red herring, Donne seems to feel, which, through its acquiescence to the demands of the natural reason, unnecessarily confuses and complicates an otherwise straightforward God-talk assertion. Luther, to put it yet another way, tries to accommodate a genuine Christian mystery to the natural law with an inevitable religiously-demeaning consequence.

"Immanuel, Christ with us" is a sacred shibboleth which perhaps might help characterize for us some of the hidden difficulties of the literary interpretation and criticism of sermon texts. I say this because Donne himself uses it to identify those in his congregation who will truly understand what is said — those he calls "worthy hearer[s]" (VI, 8, 613). There are apparently two parts to his auditory, as he sees it, which seem to correspond to what Protestantism has been pleased to call the "visible" and the "invisible" Church. The invisible Church of true believers, we may assume, are those who not only can say *"Immanuel, Christ with us,"* but are also those who "hear" the Word of God as it is dynamically present during the sermon event. "[God] sheds himselfe from my mouth, upon the whole auditory here" (VI, 8, 608-9), says Donne. "The grace of our Lord Iesus Christ be with you, and remaine with you all; . . . I can bring it so neare; but onely the worthy hearer . . . can call this Lord, this Jesus, this Christ, *Immanuel, God with us"* (VI, 8, 610-15). Donne can produce the Word of God, but he cannot force the individual listener in the pew to hear it.

What we are finally left with, it seems to me, is a form of expression in Donne's preaching which communicates not so much on two *levels*, but simultaneously within two different logical contexts. The sermon, in other words, depending upon the "worthiness" of the hearer, can be heard two ways: it can be heard as theological instruction and moral exhortation, or it can be heard as God-talk — as a speech-event during which religious discernment precipitates commitment. It is a form of expression which certainly recalls David Crystal's observation, previously quoted in Chapter Eight, that religious language is hospitable to interpretation on "two independent planes" which "ultimately conflate in the central notion 'God,' but at any one time either of the alternative modes of interpretation may be referred to." The practical obligation of Donne's preaching, then, in terms of religious utility, would be to cultivate with whatever means and to whatever extent possible a climate of logical flexibility within the individual members of his congregation, so that they might be made open to the dynamic potentiality of the Word of God as it is "shed" from Donne's mouth. The sermon, in other words, functions according to the identical strategy we have traced in the poetic devotion in the sense that it virtually manipulates the devotee into a state of consciousness receptive to an awareness of the presence of God.

As we have seen in past chapters, this communicative strategy — the strategy of virtually all literary God-talk — produces a very distinctive, yet difficult to describe, style. With its logical impropriety, its resistance to traditional patterns of conduct, its exploitation of positive ambiguity for hermeneutical potential, and its overall commitment to a non-empirical logical authority, God-talk inevitably inspires bafflement, confusion, mystery and a sense of the half-understood. Logan Pearsall Smith, for example, recognizing in Donne's sermons "something baffling and enigmatic which still eludes our last analysis," becomes somewhat enigmatic himself when he suggests that "Donne is often saying something else, something poignant and personal, and yet, in the end, incommunicable to us."[12] T.S. Eliot, suggesting that "incommunicableness" may also be merely the "vague and the unformed," senses an "impure motive" in Donne's preaching, and sees in Donne himself "a little of the religious spellbinder, the Reverend Billy Sunday of his time, the fleshcreeper, the sorcerer of emotional orgy."[13] William Mueller contends that "at least a part of that quality which Mr. Eliot defines as 'emotional orgy' can be explained by Donne's existential view of God."[14] The debate goes on.

Without directly challenging the validity of any of the many helpful explanations of the distinctiveness of Donne's preaching style, I would like to conclude with the suggestion that that "distinctiveness" may not be entirely, nor even largely, the consequence of Donne's personality, his *"goût pour la vie spirituelle,"* or his literary ingenuity, but the consequence, rather, of a well-

12. *John Donne: Sermons; Selected Passages,* ed. Logan Pearsall Smith (Oxford, 1919), p. xxxv.

13. "Lancelot Andrewes," *Selected Essays,* 2nd ed. (London, 1934), pp. 342-43.

14. *John Donne: Preacher* (Princeton University Press, 1962), p. 241.

functioning, superbly-rendered God-talk. Perhaps our most fruitful approach to the celebrated enigma of Donne's sermons may be simply to understand them not as specimens of religious art, but as religious instruments, that we become, in a word, "worthy hearers."

INDEX OF NAMES AND TITLES